God's Big Coast

ROY GETMAN

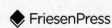

FriesenPress

Suite 300 - 990 Fort St
Victoria, BC, V8V 3K2
Canada

www.friesenpress.com

ISBN
978-1-5255-6003-3 (Hardcover)
978-1-5255-6004-0 (Paperback)
978-1-5255-6005-7 (eBook)

1. TRAVEL, UNITED STATES, WEST, PACIFIC (AK, CA, HI, NV, OR, WA)

Distributed to the trade by The Ingram Book Company

Dedicated to Rachel and our sons Paul and Jim
and my near and dear coastal family

Table of Contents

Overview

THIS BOOK IS a collection of stories—some humorous, some touchingly sad—originally written for the author's sons and scripted here for a wider audience. His life began as a hillbilly boy in Oregon. That dramatically changed at age nine when he made his first trip to Alaska by boat. The various chapters talk about those earliest years (and later experiences) in boat shops, with Boeing, working on tugs, a number of small craft voyages, and his experience as a designer and builder, and his last forty-five years as missionary and mission-boat skipper.

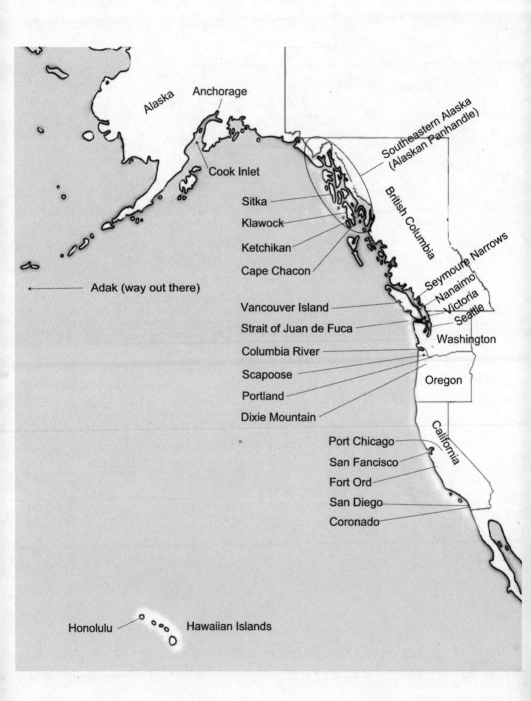

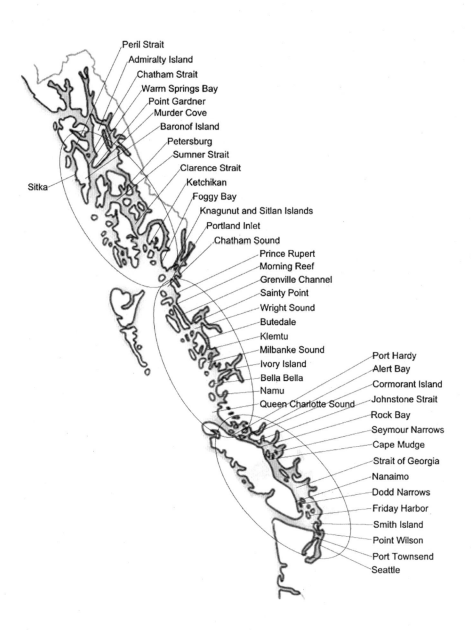

Peril Strait
Admiralty Island
Chatham Strait
Warm Springs Bay
Point Gardner
Murder Cove
Baronof Island
Petersburg
Sumner Strait
Clarence Strait
Ketchikan
Foggy Bay
Knagunut and Sitlan Islands
Portland Inlet
Chatham Sound
Sitka
Prince Rupert
Morning Reef
Grenville Channel
Sainty Point
Wright Sound
Butedale
Klemtu
Milbanke Sound
Ivory Island
Bella Bella
Namu
Queen Charlotte Sound
Port Hardy
Alert Bay
Cormorant Island
Johnstone Strait
Rock Bay
Seymour Narrows
Cape Mudge
Strait of Georgia
Nanaimo
Dodd Narrows
Friday Harbor
Smith Island
Point Wilson
Port Townsend
Seattle

Foreword

My first trip to Alaska was on the ship *Gleaner,* which you see here. Fresh out of the hills of Oregon, one whiff of ocean air mixed with the smell of diesel smoke set the course for the rest of my life.

Coastal people and boaters will readily identify with moving about on the sea, and lovers of West Coast history will find what is written to be fascinating and informative.

No great accuracy is assured; most information was simply taken from memories and my own perceptions. The arrangement of writing is largely chronological, but not always. The first chapter, for example, takes place during my awkward teen years. First, though, let me tell you a bit about where I came from.

Introduction

MY FATHER'S MISSOURI drawl, slow talk, and even his singing voice was much like Johnny Cash. He was perhaps fourteen when he met my mother-to-be in Minnesota. She was from a cheese-making family in Wisconsin.

They married just as America was plunged into the most severe economic time in its history, known as the Great Depression. They soon moved to Oregon where my father could make a living in sawmilling.

Things changed after the start of World War II when both of my parents went to work at a shipyard in Portland, Oregon. That went on for a few years until my father returned to logging and sawmilling.

Seeing potential for forest industries in Alaska, Dad traveled there by steamship in 1947 and had a serious look. The following year, he bought a ship, named it *Gleaner,* and in 1949, our family made the trip to Ketchikan.

A few years later, and still with the ship, we moved to the remote village of Klawock on the outer coast of Prince of Wales Island, Alaska, where the ship was outfitted as a floating hospital. I continued in school and graduated from grade 8 in the village.

The first chapter, *Fat F in Science,* starts just days after leaving the village, as a passenger on a fish packer on its way to Seattle, to start into grade 9.

ꝼat F in Science

I STOOD ON deck of the sturdy fish packer *Lorelei II* as she plowed her way southward. The steady purr of the engine, the sound of water rushing past the hull, the warmth and aroma of late-summer air, and the beauty of sculpted rocks along the shore… It was all was so beautiful; the colors and shadows were intensified by the low rays of evening. One of the guys turned to leave the deck, saying, "It looks like we'll be in Seattle tomorrow afternoon." I remained outside in the warm air as the sun slowly dipped below the horizon.

That was the third of September, 1953, the fourth day out of Alaska, and nine days before my fourteenth birthday.

Days later, I was sitting in a classroom at Jane Adams Junior High with about thirty grade 9 students and a teacher whose talk made little sense. People in that world rattle out whole sentences as one long word.

I was seated at my desk when an alarming rumble was heard, and it continued to grow louder, almost shaking the classroom! I ran to the window and gazed out as a heavy truck and trailer passed by.

My heart was still pounding when I turned to sit down. All classroom eyes were on me: the weird kid who nearly panicked at the sound of a passing vehicle.

Everyone laughed.

Something embarrassing happened every day at school; nothing came out right when I tried to answer the teacher.

I tried to hide the hurt of the student's mirth.

The boys seemed to know *everything* about cars, and I had no connection. Boys and girls had their friends in the hallway, and on school grounds, and on the school bus, and I had no one.

My guardian home was with Frank and Betty Dale and their five children. Jimmy, about a year and a half younger and skinny as a stick, was a nice kid, with an Adam's apple that was his most prominent feature.

He began teaching me about cars; his hobby was to collect new car brochures that he happily shared with me. Between his prompting and those printed pages, I came to realize that the boys at school didn't actually know much of what they talked about; none were old enough to drive.

School continued as a dread. All came to light at report-card time: D in Washington State History and F in everything else except Phys Ed and Band.

The science teacher, a wholesome Scandinavian-looking fellow with blond hair scrupulously combed to one side, was surprised to learn about my background as he talked with Frank and Betty about the F in Science.

I sat expressionless, attempting to hide my shame, and then he turned to me in an effort to prompt *some* kind of response. Sensing that he truly wanted to know what had gone wrong, I told him that I couldn't understand his big words and fast talk.

He sat speechless for several moments, and then in most deliberate tones, said, "I will slow down, explain everything carefully, and *be sure* you understand."

Interviews continued that Saturday with each of the teachers. Mrs. Tanner, a lovely and polite professional person, showed no sympathy for my struggle in Washington State History. It was beyond her to understand that she was looking at a kid who had never heard of a parking meter, a mountain pass, or any place surrounding Seattle.

I was again in the science classroom on Monday. The teacher carried on as usual, talking like a machine gun while punching out half-diagrams on the chalkboard. Then his eyes met mine. He went silent, erased everything, and said, "Let's start again."

With that, he continued, but this time, speaking slowly and deliberately, he explained his words and drew his diagrams carefully and fully.

Seeing that *he* cared, I did too, and an A in Science proved it on the next report card.

That remained the case through the remainder of the school year: A's in Science, B's in Algebra, C's in everything else except Washington State History, which was always a D.

Mrs. Tanner, bless you for those hopeful Ds. I memorized the counties, the state flower, and the motto "Keep Washington Green."

Thinking about it now, Mrs. Tanner usually wore something green.

A Long Way Home

TURNING THAT F into an A helped restore my confidence, and so did the realization that the boys were only trying to be "cool," but I still felt glaringly out of place. Nothing alleviated my longing for the coastal life, the ship *Gleaner*, my parents, and familiar things.

Lake Union and the Ship Canal was a distance from the Dales's place, and on a Saturday, I could run and walk those miles pretty fast to get there. A lot of surplus floating equipment was moored at Lake Union, and being less than ten years after the war, there was a lingering aroma that smelled very much like *Gleaner*: a stale mix of diesel fuel, oil-based paints, and musty cordage. It was like perfume to me.

I moved from pier to pier, drinking in the fragrance before heading back. The sad effect was that I would return to the house feeling more different, more homesick, and more alone than ever.

Gleaner arrived in Seattle that next June for an extensive facelift at Seattle's Fisherman's Terminal facilities. It felt good to be back on the ship and in my regular quarters. That arrangement ended when *Gleaner* returned to Alaska in August.

I was then off to southern California to live with

my oldest brother, Frank, his wife, Nancy, and their little one, Marileen. Theirs was a nice apartment off Orange Avenue in Coronado, where I could easily walk to Coronado High for grade 10.

Frank was in the navy, and in a situation where he could go to work each day and return home in time for supper.

Outside the apartment was an ornamental date palm; its dates were stunted and mealy, but to me (always hungry), they were sweet and satisfying. I would often do my homework sitting in a garden chair, nibbling away at the chewy fruit.

The school had the finest of everything and the best of teachers, reminding me of a naval academy. Most of the students were from navy families and familiar with different parts of the world, which made them sensitive and respectful of differing cultural influences.

Fitting in was easy, and I made friends with two other boys. When talking about our fathers, I said that mine operated a hospital ship in Alaska. One boy was surprised, because his father was one of the captains on the ferries that ran between San Diego and Coronado. The second boy was reluctant to say *anything* about his father, but after some urging, he shook his head in a way that seemed to say, "I was told not to talk about my father," and then said that his father was captain of the aircraft carrier *Hornet*, presently docked in San Diego.

Things changed partway through the school year when Frank was posted to a ship more or less permanently based a distance up the Sacramento River, halfway up the state. We moved to the nearby community of Port Chicago. Again, he reported for duty on the ship each day and was home for supper. I was enrolled at Concord High and rode the school bus.

We received news from Alaska in May saying that clinic facilities in Klawock were now in full operation, and that *Gleaner* was retired from medical service. The ship was now moored at Mount Edgecombe, a community and former air station adjoining Sitka on Baronof Island.

That was good news to me, as it meant I could join the ship, be with my parents, and continue high school in Sitka in the fall. I mailed my few possessions to my parents in anticipation of hitchhiking home when the present school year ended.

Why hitchhike? Neither my brother, on navy pay, nor my parents, just off the medical mission field, were in a position to help financially. I had thirty-five dollars and some change and was confident I could get to Seattle and find a boat going to Alaska.

Mine was a strange emotion after saying goodbye to Frank and Nancy and eighteen-month-old Marileen, and walking to a place where I could get a ride.

After several rides, it was getting dark when dropped off at some lonely place in the forested high country of northern California where an icy wind wafted through the trees.

Few vehicles were continuing over the mountain pass at that hour and fading daylight made the chance of a ride unlikely. I turned and started back, hoping to find a spot that offered better prospects.

After no more than half a mile, I came to a well-lit tavern where a trucker asked if I was heading north. He said that his rig was heavy and slow, but if I didn't mind the grind, I was most welcome to ride with him.

The next hours were spent in the warm cab with a most kindly spoken man who used hands and feet to shift gears and wrestle the steering wheel of a truck hauling seventy thousand pounds of steel through the tortuous twists of a mountain highway leading eventually into Oregon.

It was morning when he pulled off, saying he needed to turn onto another highway to deliver the steel. He thanked me, saying how much easier it had been to drive through the night having company.

I continued hitchhiking, and eventually arrived at a place on the north side of Seattle within walking distance of the Dale family home. Betty opened the door, and in moments, the family gathered as if greeting a big brother just home.

In the days that followed, I walked to Fisherman's Terminal and spoke with fellows on a New England Fish Company tender who said they were planning to leave within the week.

The vessel's master—a round-faced fellow with a ball cap that covered a notably high forehead—had no objection to me joining his vessel but said he needed to check with his company for permission.

When they learned that I was under sixteen, and fearing legal liability, his office advised against it. It was truly a letdown, especially felt a few days later as I stood on the pier letting lines go as the vessel untied and left.

That same day, I came across some young fellows readying a small seine boat, *Ira*, for its trip to Alaska. The crew consisted of the owner's two sons and two other fellows. One was from Chicago, and up to that time, he had never been near a boat. The older son was doing all the work, as he had commercially fished with his father before.

I pitched in easily with him since it was all familiar. I had fished on the side-rigged vessel *Vongee* and the ground-line fishing vessel *Frolic* during the summer of 1953.

The boy's father—*Ira*'s owner—was off in a pickup truck. When he returned, the son asked if I could go with them to Ketchikan. The father quizzed me on my intent, and when satisfied, explained that he intended to travel around the clock.

Ira was slow. The son and I ran it the greater portion of those long days and nights to Ketchikan, and upon arrival, we tied in Thomas Basin. It was early afternoon when I said goodbye to all and walked to the Marine View Hotel, securing a four-dollar room with its bathroom down the hall. I wanted to go straight to bed but knew there was more to be done.

This was before Alaska ferries, and the probability of any boat traveling from Ketchikan to Sitka was highly unlikely.

I walked to the Ellis Air Lines office and spoke with a woman behind the counter, explaining that I could not afford a plane ticket but could square up once I was back home with my parents.

A man who was handling boxes behind the lady overheard the conversation, turned directly to me, and said, "Just be here at eight in the morning, and we'll worry about a ticket some other time."

The man was likely Bob Ellis, owner of the outfit. He and all the southeast Alaska pilots knew *Gleaner*. They often delivered mail no matter where the ship was, and he'd likely figured out who I was and why I was trying to get home to Sitka. His kind gesture speaks of the understanding that made (and still makes) Alaska uniquely Alaska.

Back again at the hotel that same afternoon, I promptly fell into a sound sleep. My first thought upon waking was that it was morning, but then had second thoughts. In Alaska in June, one can't tell the difference between 6:00 a.m. and 6:00 p.m.

Being too shy to ask, I went out onto the street to see if I could figure it out. People were everywhere, but in Alaska in June, you can't go by that. I looked into the window of a restaurant, trying to see if people were eating breakfast or supper. It was only when I saw people lined up for the movie *Dial M for Murder* that I knew it *had* to be evening, so I returned to the hotel, went to bed, had a good sleep, and caught the 8:00 a.m. flight the next morning.

I was aboard *Gleaner* and with my parents shortly after landing.

Shot in the Belly

IT WAS GOOD being with my parents again on *Gleaner* and pitching in with my dad. Daily care of the craft seemed right and normal.

That work continued through the summer. Having a carpenter shop on the aft deck was handy to the vessel's needs but also for jobs I could do on other boats from time to time, which put a few dollars in my pocket.

Going into high school for grade 11 that September was easy, since Sitka kids were notably open and friendly.

The concept of an "allowance" had yet to be discovered when I was young. If a child wanted money, he did something to earn it. I took over cleaning the local Mount Edgecombe Post Office for someone who was away for the winter. Having a key to get in made it possible to do the work in the early morning hours before school.

The following spring, in 1956, I got an after-school job as a flunky at the Alaska Pioneer Home: three levels of care ranging from assisted living up to final breath.

One day, I was sent to get something in the cavernous basement. I walked the poorly lit hallway and found what I *thought* was the right door. Feeling the wall for a light switch, and being unable to find it, I stood inside the room in darkness, waiting for my eyes to adjust. They did. When I realized I was in the morgue, standing at the feet of a body, I left, looking no further for the light switch.

In 1957, seventeen young men and three young women graduated from Sitka High, with mixed emotions. Ours was a celebration of completion, sobered by the reality that we all would soon be off into full-time life.

I immediately went to work with a crew at the nearby Sheldon Jackson College—oldest institution of higher learning in Alaska, named in honor of early missionary and educator Rev. Sheldon Jackson. My first job was with a team replacing shingles on the gym, which meant a lot of shingles. Being afraid of heights, it came as a relief to be assigned to work with a carpenter preparing for the construction of a new administration building.

Trenches needed to be dug for putting in cement footings, and layers of clay and sandstone had to be loosed by pickaxe before shoveling could be done.

That work went on through the whole month of August and into September during a stretch when it rained every day. At times, there was as much bailing as picking and shoveling.

I turned eighteen on the twelfth of September, and that meant it was time to report for military duty.

I was soon off to Fort Ord, California for six months of intensive army training, and it was there that I became acquainted with drill sergeants, poison oak, and snoose (chewing tobacco).

I was with a fellow soldier—the name BENDER sewn on his green fatigues—at the army-base bus depot, standing under a long porch roof held up by steel-pipe stanchions. Bender reached into his shirt pocket and pulled out a round container. I watched as he opened its lid, took a pinch of something, and put it in his mouth.

Seeing me watching, he asked, "Want some?"

"What is it?" I questioned.

"Copenhagen," he answered.

"What do I do with it?"

"Here, I'll show you," he said, taking a pinch and shoved it in behind his lower lip.

So that's what I did too.

Just then, Bender met an old friend and the two were quickly engrossed in conversation. Having swallowed some of the black juice (snoose), I became dizzy and began sliding down the pipe stanchion I was hanging on to. Feeling greatly nauseated—Lord have mercy—and seeing a big dumpster across the street, I crossed over, opened its steel door, leaned in, and just that fast, all was goodbye Copenhagen and hello relief, the beginning and end of my snoosing.

Infantry training came first, which was normal for anyone in the army. It teaches how to legally do for one's country what would be mighty wrong on one's own. More seriously, it teaches young men that there is a much greater authority than oneself.

Most all the instructors were veterans of World War II,  intent on building the next generation of fighting men that could hold, at *any cost,* the line of freedom we so enjoy and take for granted today.

We went through many exercises during those first months. One foggy night found us soldiers in foxholes expecting an enemy invasion. It was only for training purposes, but by skillful indoctrination, it seemed very real. Meanwhile, I was suffering indigestion after eating supper rations with nothing to drink. The canteen on my belt had been empty of water since early afternoon.

A distant cry was heard in the wee hours.

"Who goes there?" Silence.

Seconds later and pitched higher, "Who goes there?"

Again, silence. Then a third time, "Who goes there?"

A gun shot echoed across the valley, and then all returned to silence, clammy fog, and indigestion.

It was a long night.

The next morning in the bleachers, soldiers learned that an officer who was grading the exercise, assuming himself to be exempt from the action, ignored the "Who goes there?" challenge from the soldier and was shot. Not dead, though. The rifle was loaded with blanks, but even so, the force of the blast blackened his coat and burned his belly.

I was eventually placed in specialized training, where we learned to operate machines able to transmit coded messages in battle conditions, and also to break enemy codes.

One training exercise taught how to hurriedly set up a battlefield operations outpost, complete with swiftly laid wires leading to dozens of remote phone stations. All was made to seem very real.

Most things learned in those intensive months of army training served in some relevant way later on in life. However, one thing I became good at but have so far never needed to know was how to quickly draw a rifle from the hip and shoot a surprise plywood pop-up person.

Getting home to Alaska after those months in training was interesting. First, we were taken by train to Fort Lewis, Washington. From there, soldiers were posted to duty abroad.

Word soon got around though that three of us were not being posted, but *going home* to Alaska—Alaska in those days was considered "overseas." We were slated to go by troop ship to Adak. Adak? Adak is part of Alaska, but so far out on the Aleutian chain that one needs to unfold pages in the atlas to find it.

Fortunately, there was a change of plans. We three were called out from the others and bused to nearby McChord Air Force Base and told we'd be *flying* to Anchorage. Anchorage is also a long way from Sitka, but nothing like end-of-the world Adak. Who knows how anyone would ever get from Adak to Sitka?

Airplanes were relatively slow in those days, allowing time to walk around inside and socialize. Other soldiers on the plane gathered around the three of us asking questions. They found it difficult to grasp that Alaska, at least parts of it, was a nearly normal place.

The aircraft landed in a mist of fine snow at Elmendorf Field, where soldiers and gear were transferred to utilitarian bus-like vehicles. The caravan was soon off into a world of white, until things came to an abrupt but lengthy halt while waiting for a confused moose standing in the way. All earlier attempts to convince that Alaska was a nearly normal place were suddenly and completely negated.

Two days and two flights later, I was again on the ship *Gleaner* and glad to be home.

The Eye Splice

WHAT WAS "NORMAL life" in my childhood was unlike anything normal to others growing up. Early years on a ship meant chores were different. Splicing and maintaining ship's mooring lines was a task inherited at about age twelve or thirteen, when my older brothers left home.

Rope was made from natural fibers in those days, and was easily chaffed or broken. My job was to salvage lengths by cutting out bad sections and rejoining the ends, or when needed, making up new lines with an eye splice on one end and a back splice on the other.

Being home on *Gleaner* after the army meant that I was again cleaning, scraping, painting, and attending to the care of mooring lines—all familiar things and helpful to Dad.

Duty to my country continued as weekly Army Reserve meetings at the local armory in Sitka. Each year, that military unit went on a two-week bivouac at Fort Richardson, outside of Anchorage, and part of training included guard duty.

After memorizing a list of what every soldier is *never* to forget, I was taken by truck to some lonely place and dropped off. Except for a wire fence in the vehicle's headlights, I had no idea where I was or what I was to be guarding, and before I could ask, the truck was gone.

It was one of those rare pitch-black nights and horribly cold. Of the list earlier memorized, I wondered what applied. I felt around and found the wire-mesh fence and leaned my rifle against it, and then crouching down, I flared the lower edge of my heavy wool trench coat out and pulled my arms, hands, and head in, to make sort of a tent—I'd heard of Eskimos surviving through the night in their sealskin parkas that way.

Suddenly, the silence was broken by the sound of footsteps. I poked my head out and stood, not making a sound, while feeling for the rifle. The night returned to silence ... silence ... long silence. Then I heard footsteps again. By then, I had the rifle in my hands—it's a court martial offence not to have your rifle—but then, all returned to silence and cold.

Again, and clearly, I heard the snap of frozen twigs under the weight of *somebody's* feet. Could this be foul play? Was the army testing my vigilance?

Finally, oh finally, there came the faintest hint of morning's light and the silhouette of a nearby moose.

I guess they sleep standing up.

Being part of the Army Reserves continued when I left Alaska to attend college in Seattle. In that case, I was able to join a U.S. Army floating-craft outfit. The army had all kinds of floating stuff during the war but had let go of most of it as surplus afterwards. They had buildings on the shore of Lake Washington, where meetings were held, and a tug that was sometimes used for training. Each summer—two summers in a row in my case—the whole bunch of us flew to southern California for training, using (would you believe) navy equipment.

On one such outing, our unit flew to Los Angeles then boarded a chartered flight for the leg to San Diego. Except for the flight crew, all of us were soldiers. Some of the guys began calling out to the stewardesses, "Can we have a Coke or something?"

One of them explained that the flight was short and there was not sufficient time to distribute drinks "unless we have some help."

An officer poked me in the back and said, "Give them a hand."

I did, and all went smoothly, and before the plane landed, one of the stewardesses attached an attractive golden pin on my uniform—wings on a circle with writing. I always wore it on my class-A uniform after that, along with a few other medals earned in training. Eyes often studied it, but no one ever asked, and no one got close enough to read the tiny words in the circle: "Junior Stewardess."

During my first time in California with that unit, I operated a fifty-six-foot-long navy landing craft, LCM for short. Having been around boats and boat-handling situations since childhood, I had no difficulty operating the craft, and that included walking it sideways, exactly what was required in one case.

The LCM was brought up to the side of a cargo ship, one engine pushing ahead, the other astern, rudders hard over, as oil drums were lowered. Throttles were varied to move the LCM forward or back on the side of the ship to be sure the weight of each sling load was positioned well forward and exactly where they should go in the craft's open hold.

Next in that assignment was to rally off a specified practice beach with nine other landing crafts: a beach-assault exercise. All boats were loaded with soldiers with rifles and bayonets. My LCM had only a few soldiers and the oil drums.

Ten flag persons stood on the beach—each craft was to watch the equivalent flagger for precise beaching instructions. No particular instruction was needed on this stretch of sand, such as might be the case in a combat zone where there could be reefs or sunken wreckage.

All landing crafts roared to life as soon as the ten flags were dipped, and headed directly for their flagger.

I had earlier practiced on that stretch and knew that a submerged sandbar ran parallel to the beach some distance off the shore, and as it turned out, nine of the landing crafts got hung up on it. Some were able to squirm around and get in a little closer, but most of the soldiers had to wade in—some up to their chests while holding rifles above their heads. My LCM, loaded as it was, flattened out on a plane, never touched the sandbar, and slid so far up the sand that the flagger had to run. A bulldozer was brought in to get the craft back in the water.

Everyone had eaten supper by the time our LCM got back. I was told to report to the OP. I dreaded the lecture I'd be getting. The officer behind the desk told me to sit down. I did. He then explained that he had been in a stand watching the whole operation, and that my landing was like a landing *should* be: delivering men and cargo where it was needed. He then added, "In wartime, nobody cares about getting a landing craft off again."

Our unit was again in Coronado/San Diego the next year. This time, I was put with navy guys on a one hundred-seventy-three foot-long water tender. Being army, I was largely treated as a freak by the navy guys.

The man in charge—"Chief," they called him—was a heavily built fellow with a foghorn voice. One morning, while having breakfast in the galley, he announced that everyone would be splicing lines, and sure enough, when going out on the foredeck, there were about a dozen cut-to-length, three-strand manila lines stretched out ready for the exercise.

The men were told to team up by twos, find an end, and splice an eye. No one joined me, so I picked up the tools that were there for splicing and went to work. The line, although very large, was surprisingly soft and cooperative. After completing the tucks, including a nice taper, I stood up and rolled the new splice under my foot to make it round and smooth.

Looking around, I was surprised that no one else had finished, and some were still struggling even to get started. I suddenly sensed a presence behind me and turned around. It was Chief, and he had a mean look on his face as he bent over, picked up my spliced end, and like a weightlifter, raised it high above his head.

When all eyes were on him, he bellowed (in a most disdainful voice) at his own men, "Look, you guys; the only one that knows how to splice is the army!"

The War Years

I WAS BORN in Oregon in September of 1939, at about the same time World War II was born in Europe. Our family home was a log cabin with a dirt floor on Dixie Mountain.

I recall that cabin not from when I was a baby but a little later, when George and Clara Long lived there. They had an ashtray that looked like a little rubber tire. They'd dump the ashes out so I could play with it.

Now fast forward your mind to a time, not long ago, when an odd-shaped envelope arrived in the mail. Inside was a computer disk with a collection of scanned family photos. I stuck it in the drive of my desktop computer and began looking at the images one by one, on its high-resolution screen, and suddenly, there were George and Clara, sitting as they always did at the kitchen table.

I zoomed in to see if the ashtray was still there, and it was! *Whoa, this is too real,* I thought, as I shook my head. It took some moments to regain myself. That was seventy-five years ago!

World War II started in 1939, but America stayed out of it until its naval base at Pearl Harbor was attacked on December 7, 1941.

Reaction was swift. Americans from every walk of life rallied in support of leadership, and our Dixie Mountain family life was soon put on hold while both parents went to work at the Swan Island Shipyard in Portland, where T2-class oil tankers were to be built, the first of which to be named *Schenectady*—a name borrowed from the city in the State of New York.

My older siblings, Frank, Byrl, and LuAnn, were placed with different families, while I remained with my parents and was put in the shipyard nursery.

Mothers seldom worked outside the home prior to that time in American history, but young men were off to war and laborers were few, so women—married and unmarried—quickly learned the needed skills. My mother, for example, excelled as a pipe welder.

The day came, October 24, 1942, when the newly constructed *Schenectady* was to be launched. It was a day of celebration and one of my earliest recollections. It started as a big picnic, and then the ship was opened for viewing. I was half carried up steel stairs to its deck by the hands of my oldest brother, boosted along with the moving crowd through corridors, and up more stairs to a place where we emerged into open air. I was lifted up to see the ground far below. My first response was fright until I realized that I was looking down at people moving about far below.

The crowd later assembled on the ground to watch the launch. After speeches and some amount of fanfare, an extravagantly dressed Miss Priss stepped up, ready to christen the ship by breaking a bottle of champagne on its bow as soon as it began to move.

Blocks were released, and the ship began ever so slowly to slide down the slipway. She banged the bottle daintily about, and after many failed attempts, a fellow stepped up, took it from her hands, and smashed it properly.

My mother later told me what she had been thinking at the time: *If I ever have a chance to christen a ship, I'll do the job right the first time.*

Jump ahead thirty-seven years (momentarily) to June 1, 1980, when Mom was asked to christen the Coastal Missions Society's first mission vessel, *Coastal Messenger*—an event that attracted a sizable crowd in picturesque Victoria Harbour in front of the famed Empress Hotel.

The neck of the Canada Dry bottle had been carefully wrapped with tape, to prevent the possible breaking of glass in her hand. It was also enshrouded with delicate white netting with red, blue, and gold ribbons tied around the top.

After speeches, and the sounds of a rousing brass band, she took position on the float close to the nose of the ship, and when prompted, took hold of the bottle with both hands, hauled back, and swung as if batting a home run. A great cheer went up as she stepped back, licking the spray from her lips and looking enormously self-satisfied with what she'd just done.

Let's go back in time to talk about that first T2 tanker *Schenectady* my mother had helped to build. She once told me of the worst day in her life: January 16, 1943. It was a cold and miserable day in Portland. The ship was tied at the shipyard. Water had been pumped into both ends for stress testing. Suddenly and without warning, there was the most horrid sound of wrenching steel, loud enough to be heard for miles, as the hull cracked in two all the way down to its bottom plating.

Both ends settled on the bottom of the river. The split middle portion floated up and remained afloat. No one was injured, but she said it was like the combined passing of a loved one and the loss of all that had gone into building the ship. What had gone wrong? There were speculations and investigations and perhaps some conclusions. Whatever the cause, the ship was fixed, more tankers were built, and the war continued and was eventually won.

America was in great need of railroad ties, and Dad knew how to make them, so my parents left shipbuilding and returned to Dixie Mountain.

Home by then was a framed house a mile or two from the earlier log cabin. Our family mailbox, Route 1, Box 90, sat on a wooden post along with a few others at a wide spot in the gravel road, leading along the ridge of the mountain. One could look out on a clear day and see several significant peaks: Mount Adams, Mount Hood, Mount Saint Helens, and Mount Jefferson.

This time, rather than work for somebody else, my father gathered a crew and set up his own milling and logging operation.

His mill was advanced for its time. The rollers for moving railroad ties and other lumber were electrically powered. Cutoff saws were also electric. Power came from a big slow-turning Fairbanks Morris diesel engine, coupled to a sizable generator a short distance away.

Mother's days were filled with the cares of the house and home, farm animals, chickens, and gardening. Seeing her in that role, one would never have guessed her wide range of abilities.

Logging was done from a spar tree on a peak rigged in typical fashion. Dad was hauled to the top on a straw line one day, and the operator of the machine clumsily pulled him into the block at the top. Nothing broke and my father was okay, but always after that, he insisted that Mother operate the machinery at the bottom.

It was summer 1945, and I was five when my mother, standing in the living room of the house, called me to her side. She was holding a newspaper, and by her expression and watery eyes, I knew that what she was going to say was important. She lowered the paper and pointed out a blurred image on the page.

"I want you to remember this man," she gently lectured. "His name is Eisenhower; he's a good man."

Although too young to comprehend what she was telling me at the time, the photo and the name Eisenhower were permanently imprinted. Looking back, I'm quite certain that she had just read that the war had ended. In any case, this was General Dwight D. Eisenhower of the American forces, who later became President of the United States. Now, all these decades later, history likely agrees he was a "good man."

ᴾenciled Elephant

MY MOTHER SWALLOWED a pencil before I was born, and I arrived with it in my hand. That's not true, of course, but having a compulsion to draw did come early—not so much as works of art but mainly, mostly, and merely as doodles or to communicate what was hard to put into words.

Drawing while growing up seemed to be as much a bane as a benefit. When going to school, for example, I adorned margins of workbooks and textbooks with aimless scribbles, widgets, gizmos, and gadgets and got in trouble for it.

A psychologist may read this book and come up with a label, such as CDS (Compulsive Drawing Syndrome) or something like that. For some reason, mindless drawing has always made listening, concentrating, and learning easier for me. The inclination and habit, good or bad, was (and is) incurable.

My quarters inside *Gleaner* were just forward of the ammunition locker, where it was possible to observe the specialized fittings where wires and pipes passed through the watertight steel bulkhead. I found such things fascinating, and around age twelve began sketching in a fashion that is now computerized and called "layers." That kind of drawing has no artistic interest but did assist 3D thinking.

When it came to art, I tried oil painting in my twenties, but found it messy and smelly, and the brushes hard to clean. In any case, I was seldom pleased with the outcomes. There was one exception. While thumbing through a magazine, I came upon a photo that showed men on the deck of a fishing schooner. Attention was drawn to the weatherworn face of a man in oilskins. The face was only the size of a thumbnail but was enough to inspire a life-size portrait on canvas that even now hangs in its frame above our fireplace.

I also did a number of half-penned, half-brushed India ink drawings. The one shown here is a mind's view of the ocean-going tug, *Barbara Foss,* with its barge outbound in the Strait of Juan de Fuca.

Most of anything drawn was hastily sketched and soon discarded, such as this nose-to-nose submarine and whale, with hearts radiating from the whale and the caption, "Love at first echo."

There is a type of logging that calls for falling trees and getting the logs to the sea, where they can be rafted and towed to a mill. This usually calls for a sturdy boat to assist pulling the logs off the shore. Things sometimes go wrong. That, of course, is never funny at the time, but later calls for storytelling … and storytelling calls for cartooning.

I heard a fellow tell the story of running a workboat when the engine quit as it was approaching the rocky shore. He ran out on the bow with a pike pole to ward off hitting the rocks. His quick action worked, except that the handle of the pole went up his sleeve, lifted him up, and dumped him into the back

of the boat. He said that he had trouble getting the handle out. I never did draw that one.

I did, however, come up with several cartoons of things told by others—all hurriedly penned on cheap tablet paper and colored with crayons. Whenever those cartoons were brought out and shown to one who was familiar with the story, another story would be told—the making of another cartoon.

My very first drawing was an elephant like you see here. It was done long ago, when I was small enough to walk under a kitchen table. I found a pencil somewhere in the house of my mother's friend. No one was in the room when the elephant happened. When it was discovered, I realized that whoever drew it was in trouble, and being that the elephant was low on the refrigerator, it seemed to automatically incriminate me. I tried to deny it, but did agree that whoever did it was small; I said I saw him do it. That was as far as I'd admit.

Brother Frog

THERE WAS NO evidence of religion around our home when I was small—no bedtime prayers or anything like that. Good behavior was demanded. My parents were honest and wholesome, and to *do unto others as you would have them do unto you* was woven into the family fabric.

Days after World War II ended, I started school in a one-room schoolhouse at the bottom of Dixie Mountain. Miss Tenant, probably in her early twenties, was our teacher.

I suspect that a room full of lively children, grades 1 through 8, in the one classroom was too much for her. The raucous behavior of the older boys demanded most of her time and energies, so not surprising, we little ones missed learning to read.

Grade two was another five miles down the road, in the town of Scappoose. Students rode to school in an old decrepit school bus, with a jerky clutch, grinding gears, and smelly exhaust. It was a pile of junk that would likely not be allowed on the road today. None of that posed concern to me at age seven, when everything was big, exciting, and new.

I gazed around the classroom. There were placards with symbols above the chalkboards. Being curious, I asked aloud—speaking to no one in particular—what they were. A boy in a nearby desk answered, "That's the alphabet, stupid."

That same boy was with me a few days later, during the lunch break, seemingly attracted to my ignorance. A steam locomotive puffed its way along the tracks on the other side of the highway. Several box cars rolled noisily behind and eventually passed.

"Wow," I said, "I wonder where those tracks go."

"There's a whole nation out there," he replied impatiently.

"A nation… What are you talking about?"

"There's a whole nation of people, with a president and everything."

So, I asked, "Who is the president?"

"Harry Truman," he said. Then he added, "The years are numbered."

Curious, I asked, "What number is this one?"

"1947."

School children carried metal lunch containers in those days. A different boy, Victor, who lived part way up Dixie Mountain, got on the bus with only a paper bag. One day, someone asked what he had in it.

"A potato," he answered.

Some of the children laughed. One day, he was discovered having a bag with *nothing* in it, and he tried to hide the fact. This was hilariously funny to some, yet dreadfully sad to others. Those riding the bus were divided after that. Some commonly made fun of Victor and others gave him parts of their lunch.

There was a little country church a few miles along the mountain ridge. In time, my mother and older siblings began going to services there. My father stayed home, so I copied him. Later, when he decided to go, I did too.

I had no idea what church or Sunday school was about. All different ages met together at first and were then dismissed to classes according to age. I just stood there and somebody noticed and led me to a room where children were enthusiastically singing "Jesus Loves Me"—a song I'd never heard.

Some weeks later, I questioned my mother about things she couldn't answer, so she contacted the preacher. He came to the house and talked about asking Jesus into my heart, which even at that young age, I understood. The two of us knelt at the sofa, and I repeated his words as he helped me to pray. He was soon off to the kitchen and talking with my mother, but I lingered where we'd knelt, and then stood up, realizing something in my heart had indeed changed. I had no idea how permanent it would be.

Months later, an invited evangelist came to the church and held meetings several nights in a row. The fellow created quite a stir and many came to hear. He was a rather squat fellow, having no neck, and wore extremely thick glasses that greatly magnified his eyeballs, causing them to look as big as the lenses.

Men and women worked hard in those days and generally went to bed early. Adding to their day was not easy. No matter how profound his preaching, some would begin to struggle to stay awake.

Children enjoyed the singing part of each service but quickly dozed off when the sermon began. That didn't matter, because his message was for adults. Now and then, the evangelist would say loudly, "Do I hear an amen?" He sometimes had to repeat the question.

Someone would eventually answer, "Yes! Amen, brother."

Some weeks after the evangelist left, and after the regular morning service, children were playing in the bushes behind the church. I heard a distant voice call out, "Do I hear an amen?"

Off in the distance and from the opposite direction, I heard a faint reply, "Yes! Amen, Brother Frog."

Alaska Dream

MY FATHER WAS drawn to Alaska's great forest potential, so in 1947, he boarded the steamship *Prince George* and traveled north. He viewed a number of possible properties, including the site of what is now the Phillips fish plant at the town of Craig on Prince of Wales Island.

He continued logging and sawmilling in Oregon until he severely wrenched a knee while securing a load of lumber onto the bed of a truck. He spent some weeks in a Portland hospital, where he talked across beds with a man who had been on a merchant ship during the war and who taught Dad the rudiments of navigation.

Dad eventually came home, still weakened by the ordeal. One day, I noticed him limping about the front yard with a hammer, driving wooden stakes into the ground. It made no sense at the time, but I later realized that he was reinforcing what he'd learned about navigation.

Dad always moved on things, so it was not a surprise when he purchased a former U.S. Navy Subchaser in late 1948. That vessel and several others of its kind had been transferred to the Coast Guard after the war and named *Air*-Something. This one became *Air Willet.* At some point, all those vessels came up as surplus.

I first saw the ship at the Gunderson Brothers Shipyard in Portland, Oregon, in the spring of 1949. Its one-hundred-and-twelve-foot-long hull was painted glossy black and the name *"Doris K"* was boldly lettered across its stern. I was told the *K* stood for Kellogg, which was the last name of the person who had bought three of them.

The ship was promptly renamed *Gleaner,* and in time, its hull was painted white.

Gleaner was a highly advanced ship, having variable pitch propellers, smooth as silk. Understand that variable pitch doesn't use forward, neutral, and reverse. Shafts, when in gear, rotated continuously. At zero pitch, the vessel was propelled neither forward nor astern. Pitch could range up to sixty-four inches forward or up to thirty-nine inches in reverse. An operator controlled thrust according to need, which was an important feature in the case of a vessel with a lot of power. By minimizing pitch and rpm, propulsion could be applied most gently.

The galley was all electric, set up to feed its complement of twenty-seven persons. Refrigerated drinking water came from a fountain in the dining area. You just stuck a glass under the spigot and put your foot on the pedal. It makes me thirsty to think about it now.

The ship was powered by two 1,200 HP General Motors diesel engines, totaling 2,400 HP at 1800 rpm. The hull design was equally advanced—displacement starting from the bow and flattening to a fast shape toward the stern.

Being without the weight of guns and armament after the war, she was especially lively. Given throttle, she was like a big speedboat that leaned *into* her turns—a rare thing to see in a vessel over one hundred feet long.

At the cost of fuel, throttles were never opened up very long.

There was another side. With engines at a relaxed rpm, and propellers set to the right pitch, the ship sliced through the sea very efficiently, and at their most efficient cruising speed, those engines sounded like a big locomotive on a slight incline. From a distance, one could *feel* the throb of pistons in the air before hearing them—of course, I'm talking about an earlier time when one could go outside and feel nature and even hear the flight of a gull.

I assumed the ship to be part of my father's vision to move logging and sawmilling to Alaska. I'll never know if it was or not, but the mill move never happened (perhaps because of that knee injury). In the long of things, all the equipment in Oregon was sold.

The ship, however, was ready for departure in early July 1949 and tied at a marina in the Willamette River near Scappoose. On the day of departure, many Dixie Mountain folks and other friends and relatives came to say goodbye. Several brought gifts of one kind or another. One farming couple brought a two-gallon can of cream. Happenings were somewhat hectic, so the cream container was hastily placed in the deep galley sink.

The engines were started. The air was filled with acrid smoke. Mooring lines, one by one, were cast off. People standing on the float and along the shore continued to wave and call out good wishes as the craft maneuvered out and into the channel.

I had no idea those moments would be so final.

Everything familiar was forever left behind.

Memories of Oregon are now like pages from another life.

The Willamette River empties into the Columbia River a distance downstream. That first day ended at Astoria, gateway to the mighty Pacific.

A sizable ship, *Kenyon Victory*, was tied nearby. Her navigator, drawn by curiosity, came down onto the pier and was soon talking with Dad.

There were lightships in those days—ships that were anchored in strategic locations off the coast to serve as floating lighthouses. Each one transmitted its own unique radio signal for navigation purposes, and sounded a whistle when it was foggy. Fittingly, the lightship *Columbia* was stationed off the mouth of the Columbia River.

The man's visit was timely. *Gleaner* was equipped with radio direction-finding equipment, and the man's help to understand it was greatly valued. The next morning, he joined *Gleaner*, which was soon off on a training exercise out to the lightship *Columbia* and back.

Later, tied again at Astoria, someone thought to set up the cream can. Curious about its content, after all the rolling and banging in the deep sink, the lid was pried open, and BEHOLD, a big ball of butter!

Gleaner left the Columbia River the following morning and traveled up the coast of Washington. My brother, Frank, grasped using radio direction-finding equipment and used his understanding to confirm Dad's manual navigation. The ship entered the Strait of Juan de Fuca in heavy fog that persisted all the way into Port Angeles.

Continuing a few days later, we passed a distance off the city of Victoria. Distant surfaces on buildings reflected radiant white in the misty morning sun—an image indelibly imprinted like a preview of heaven in my memory to this day.

The ship anchored that afternoon in a crescent formed by the Ballenas Islands in the Strait of Georgia. The keeper of the nearby lightstation (lighthouse), assuming *Gleaner* to be a government vessel, launched the station's small boat and came to inquire. This soon became a social event where it was planned the family would visit the keeper and his wife in the evening.

It was a lovely day with time to enjoy the area. A boat was lowered to the water and rowed to a nearby beach where we explored the many colorful life forms in the shallows—clusters of blue and orange starfish. Everything was new and fascinating.

The keeper returned with the station's open boat, and our visit included climbing steps inside the light tower where a large kerosene lamp sat in the center of an array of glass prisms. Weights attached to a mechanism caused the lenses to revolve slowly around the lamp's flame, and in so doing, a concentrated beam of light was sent out over the sea to serve as a beacon for mariners.

It was getting late when Mom began playing the piano in the house. The keeper and his wife were a reserved couple, yet overjoyed to have talk, laughter, and music in their home. Some of my family joined in singing a haunting old black melody, "Lord, I wanna be a Christian, inna my heart, inna my heart..."

I sat quietly with the keeper and his wife as they listened and wept quietly.

I have reflected back over the great span of time since that evening, and the unusual nature of the occasion. Think of it: There we were, country people from Dixie Mountain, Oregon, bound for the last frontier, Alaska—then a territory. I had not the slightest hint that what I was seeing, hearing, and experiencing was a pattern and lesson. I had no idea that I would someday be a citizen of Canada and a missionary to people living under all three flags—Old Glory (flag of the U.S.), the Maple Leaf (flag of Canada), and the Big Dipper (flag of Alaska).

I am still fully influenced by those moments. Having been up and down these coasts for decades, I now conclude that the best way for a missionary to encourage is to simply visit in the name of Jesus, and when possible, share some homemade music.

Gleaner arrived at Ketchikan and tied at the City Floats. Having just come out of the hills in Oregon, we siblings wore no shoes; we'd always lived our summers that way. Ketchikan, in 1949, was accepting of oddities—and still is. Our presence only added to the color.

ꟻish Pirates

Ketchikan had numerous wooden streets and many of its houses and buildings were on pilings over the sea. Plumbing was simple. Everything drained or dropped directly into the salt water below. The arrangement worked well; the sea flushed twice a day.

Some pretty bizarre things could be seen floating around, but the water was too cold to swim in anyway. We soon learned to stay out from underneath homes and structures on pilings when moving about in a rowboat.

Weeks after arriving in Ketchikan, the ship was contracted to patrol floating fish traps owned by the Nakat Packing Company. Nakat was one of about a dozen big fish companies in the area. Several of their big traps were situated near Cape Chacon, a notably nasty part of this world's oceans, where the waters of Dixon Entrance pour out into the open Pacific in opposition to summer westerlies.

A buoyant log, attached by cable to a sizable anchor on the seafloor, had been placed just barely inside the cape to serve as a mooring for the ship when not moving about.

Fish traps amassed salmon by the tens of thousands; their efficiency for catching fish was phenomenal, and the worth of fish was great. A power scow from the cannery came and emptied the pens every few days.

Not surprising, a lot of fish piracy was going on. A trap robber (fish-pirate boat) would come alongside a floating trap and dip salmon out. The fish were then sold as if legally caught.

Trap owners were one step ahead. A stout little cabin for two was mounted on each trap, and watchers were assigned to look after everything. The weak point was that a few friendly dollars and a bottle or two of enticement could persuade watchers to go into cahoots with the pirates. *Gleaner*, having a serious patrol vessel profile, was a second-level deterrent.

Trap robbery seldom took place in broad daylight, so *Gleaner* would secure to its mooring log during the day and maintain vigil through the night.

I remember one rare day, when the sea was calm at Cape Chacon, an outboard-powered boat was lowered from the side of *Gleaner*. My brother Byrl and two others from the ship climbed in and motored off to visit fellows on a nearby fish trap. Byrl lingered with the skiff, lowered a fishing line, and soon hooked what he *thought* was the bottom of the sea. Then, realizing he had a big fish, he began tugging on the line. Those in the cabin saw what was happening and quickly came to help. They managed to get the huge halibut to the surface, but their combined weight had one side of the boat down low to the water, and when its nose touched the side of the skiff, it suddenly burst forward and into the boat.

Attention quickly turned to bailing and getting back to *Gleaner* before the creature's big tail beat the bottom out.

When at the side of *Gleaner*, the boom was swung into position and the halibut was hoisted up and out—all six feet seven inches of it.

Gleaner never actually *chased* fish pirates. Really, what would you do if you caught one? The mere presence of a patrol boat was enough.

Seeing the big grab of the traps, many otherwise-honest Alaskan fishermen resorted to unlawful things, such as fishing in the mouth of a stream. A more brutal way was to poison a stream with bluestone, which drove the salmon out where they could be caught, but it also killed the life of the stream.

Those owning seine boats could legally drop their nets, but the common complaint was that large corporations were profiting big time from Alaskan resources. Nakat, for example—a subsidiary of the Atlantic and Pacific Tea Company—had its offices in New York. Alaskans had no way to stop them, until statehood in 1959 when citizens were given a voice in such things.

Chasing fish pirates was neither necessary nor a good idea. For a start, just about everybody had a rifle and knew how to communicate with it; a Remington 30-30 was universal to the territory's language in those days.

There was also a host of nasty tricks commonly used by fish pirates. A line trailed in the wake of a pirate boat could easily entangle the propeller of a pursuing one.

One story going around was about a guy who threw a charge of dynamite off the stern of his boat with the intent of blowing up the pursuing patrol boat. The charge went off prematurely and blew the caulking out of the stern of his own boat; it had to be beached to prevent sinking.

When on its mooring with all the lights off, *Gleaner* had the advantage of being hidden by the backdrop of the cape. When a pirate boat came to the side of a trap, the ship's two big engines exploded to life as deck and other lights were set ablaze.

Atmosphere at sea sometimes causes voices and other sounds to be amplified. Such was the case one night when a pirate boat came in and tied to a trap a half-mile away. *Gleaner's* lights went on and engines came to life with a huge roar that echoed off the cape. In the momentary lull that followed, a voice wafted across the water in a tone distinct and clear: "Holy cow! The army, navy, and half the Coast Guard! Let's get outta here!"

Victor Rides Free

MOM AND MY sister LuAnn stayed in a small apartment above Thomas Basin when *Gleaner* was at the cape. I joined them in time to go to school that September, and after school, I sold newspapers. "Daily News! Ten cents!" I'd call out on the street, and on boardwalks, and in the many saloons.

Five cents a copy went to the printer, and five cents to my earnings. I could make a whole dollar on a good day after school, although admittedly, there were few good days.

There were no rules that prevented children being in bars in those days. Patrons always warmly welcomed my coming in with newspapers.

The Focsle Bar on Front Street was by far the most fascinating of all those in Ketchikan. Vented out to the sidewalk near the door, the smell of cigarette smoke and old beer was most welcoming to folks that otherwise had nothing but fresh air to breathe. The back wall was made to be a full-size, carefully constructed replica of a two-story pilothouse, complete with red and green navigation lights. When inside, one had the impression of being on the foredeck of a sizable packet (freight boat). Thick cigarette smoke gave the impression of being in fog. Shipwreck photos hung on walls surrounding—an amazing collection of smoked photography, all well framed and most interesting.

Another was the Arctic Bar out on pilings over the creek (actually more of a river), with an entrance coming in from Water Street. Some years after my selling papers there, it was swept off its legs and ended up down under the bridge. There's a new Arctic Bar in that location now.

The following spring, 1950, my brother Byrl came home with a baby seal that a fisherman had given to him, saying that the mother was dead. The little fellow generated a lot of attention down on the floats where we lived on *Gleaner,* and of course, the question came up, "What shall we name him?"

Looking into his big sorrowful eyes was like looking into the sad eyes of the boy on the school bus. My sister said, "Let's name him Victor."

Victor didn't know how to suck from a baby bottle. A fellow on a nearby fish boat said that seal nipples are flat, and that the little guy needed something flat to push against. Several things were tried but nothing worked. Everyone agreed that Victor needed to eat or he'd die.

A lady from a nearby boat said, "You'll have to put a tube down his throat."

A bottle with a soft hose was prepared with warm canned milk and water. With that, Victor was able to feed. He was kept in an open skiff on the deck of *Gleaner* and often lifted out and allowed to move around on deck. He was sometimes carried down to move about on the float, and on occasion, he was brought inside for the night.

He'd come flopping over for dinner as soon as he'd see his bottle. The fisherman said that seals need rich food, so Victor's diet was reinforced with mashed cooked fish. The man also said that seals couldn't swim by nature, and that their mothers have to teach them. Byrl and LuAnn made a leash from a small rope and put it around Victor's neck, with the plan of towing him behind a rowboat, hoping to teach him to swim. LuAnn was rowing, as Byrl gently lowered Victor into the water, but as soon as Victor felt the water supporting him, he stretched out his neck, slipped out of the rope, and sank.

The happy end was that he could swim just fine, and he loved his new freedom so much so that he did not always come home, and when he did, it was often after all of us went to bed. Dad, however, would stay up to watch, and lift him out of the water.

Victor followed Byrl when allowed. He was slow on land, so Byrl would sometimes pick him up and carry him. On one occasion, they were up on the street with Victor flopping along behind Byrl, when a taxi stopped.

The driver said, "Hop in. Where do you want to go?" Byrl thanked the man, but said that he had no money.

The driver said assertively, "Victor and anyone with him rides free."

Once on their way, the driver picked up the microphone and reported to his dispatcher, "I've got Victor here."

Bits of news about Victor hit the local Ketchikan paper from time to time. His story and a picture of LuAnn holding him appeared in the Alaska Sportsman magazine, July 1950.

As Victor grew, he also grew more independent. Rather than come home, he'd swim to a nearby floatplane hangar, slide up the incline, and sleep under a dry roof. By then, it was obvious he was eating out. We saw less and less of him as time went on.

You'd think the story would end there, but no, in the year 2000, I was on a boat in Ketchikan when a fellow arrived to show me something in the local newspaper: an article remembering Victor! Reading about something that was so real in my own life fifty years earlier left a strange feeling.

Ship and Village Life

EARLY SPRING 1951, *Gleaner* left Ketchikan, rounded Cape Chacon, and continued up the west coast of Prince of Wales Island to the village of Klawock. The trip was only one hundred and thirty nautical miles, but in those days before roads and phone communications, that move was like going to a distant land, with different people ... different everything. I never saw my friends Joe McNeil or Stanley Oaksmith or Victor again.

Another ship was there when *Gleaner* arrived. It was a planned meeting of ships having to do with something arranged on adult levels apart from my knowledge. Adult planning was not mixed with children's ideas in those days.

ROY GETMAN

Schooling during those first months was on the other ship, *Willis Shank*. My sister and the captain's daughter, Sandy, who were both around fourteen years old, became noisy, giggly, and almost always-together friends. Sandy, in one of her devilish exuberances, once stabbed my wrist with a sharp pencil. Sooty dark blood slowly filled the hole where the point was extracted, leaving an indelible reminder.

The *Willis Shank*, former U.S. Navy minesweeper, had been made into a medical mission ship that had copious quantities of surplus navy toilet paper that was freely shared. It was not like the flimsy stuff you see today that turns to nothing in your hand at a most critical moment. Its texture was somewhat like newspaper, with squares barely perforated. The reason I'm talking about this is because I could draw on it, and paper for drawing was almost impossible to get.

You may remember Jacob and the biblical account of angels going up and down a ladder into heaven. I drew Jacob's ladder leading up about five feet of toilet paper to an open hatch in heaven. Jacob was shown climbing out saying, "Don't see nobody up here." The ship's doctor saw it and went into near hysterics, almost needing medical help.

The two ships operated in team effort until later in 1951, when *Willis Shank* left for Seattle. Klawock continued as homeport for *Gleaner*, as she was by then operating as a full-fledged floating hospital, making rounds to places on the west coast of Prince of Wales Island. Meanwhile, ashore, a clinic was being built. Tuberculosis (TB) was an Alaskan epidemic at that time.

Gleaner was bright and clean and well equipped, but not always easy for patients. Imagine from a patient's view, walking to the end of a pier, going down a steep gangway to a float, and then up and onto the deck of a ship.

My mother was highly adaptable and fully competent. Any given day, when *Gleaner* was receiving patients, she could be seen in perfect white, graciously ushering people to their places, or still in white, going to the engine room and starting the larger of two diesel generators needed to operate an autoclave sterilizer. Later, after a busy day, she could be seen coming out of the darkroom with water dripping from freshly developed X-rays.

Living on a busy ship was ordinary life and home to me. The sound of a generator running or cries of a newborn baby were not unusual. Thirty-some babies were born on board.

The vessel made its regular rounds to Craig and Hydaburg and occasionally to other places, such as Waterfall. Ship movement was often in the dark and in heavy mist, rain, or snow conditions. Dad fully understood long-hand navigation.

Certain places along the coast were known to bounce a good whistle echo. Running in blindness and following his figures, he would bring the ship to a plotted position, sound the ship's whistle, begin counting seconds in his head, step out the side door, hear the echo, confirm the distance offshore, and continue on course to the next place to confirm by echo.

That, of course, was how vessels used to move up and down this coast.

He was close to exhaustion one night as the ship headed toward Hydaburg; he'd already put in a full day. Nurse Evelyn Hunter, affectionately known as Auntie Ev, wanted to be of help. She knew *nothing* about steering a ship, but this night was different. *Gleaner* was out in an open body of water, the night sky was clear, and there was a big round moon.

"Steer toward the moon," he told her, as she took the wheel. He went to his quarters and sat down to take the weight off his weary legs, not daring to close his eyes. He knew he must not fall asleep.

He sensed the ship was turning, but "So what?" he reasoned. It didn't matter. They were far from land. He sat and rested awhile then returned to the pilothouse. The moon was directly astern!

"I asked you to steer toward the moon," he said.

"Oh," she answered sweetly, "we passed *that* a long time ago."

Talking again about the village of Klawock, winters were much colder back then, and part of that was because we lived down inside the ship, often frozen in ice. Dad had a good way of preventing *Gleaner* from getting locked in completely: He'd start the engines and use the wash of propellers, one ahead and one in reverse, to break ice ahead and astern. Once free, the ship would maneuver out and cut big ice circles, pushing them out and, thus, clearing the whole harbor.

One time, during one of those ice-breaking exercises, the hull was breached. No one noticed until the next morning, when Dad noted things were not right.

Each compartment was fitted with a telephone, and one was in LuAnn's stateroom in the bow. He phoned her. Her phone was within easy reach, so she simply reached out from beneath cozy covers and answered, agreeing to check the forward bilge when she got up.

Moments later, she sprung out of bed with youthful agility and landed knee-deep in ice water. Had she landed a few inches forward of where she did, she would have gone in over her head, where the cover of a bilge access hole had floated off.

The hull was holed in the very peak. Once the water was pumped out, and a valve that isolated that compartment was closed, the ship continued through the winter without concern for the little water it carried in its nose.

Boys Will Be Boys

I WAS ENROLLED in the Klawock public school soon after *Willis Shank* left, and was the only white boy in classes at the time. I readily made friends and adjusted to the language and ways of the people.

The language was English but often skewed by phrases and expressions from the old Tlingit, and spiced with local colloquial idioms and coastal jargon. Body, facial, and hand expressions often did the talking. Friends would often come together merely to be together and not say anything.

Silence often says the most when a situation is saddest.

As said earlier, *Gleaner* was home, but when the ship was away on rounds during the school year, I stayed in fish-cannery quarters that were looked after by Dick and Dean Nelson. Dick was a knowledgeable seafaring man and Dean a lovely caring mother. Much attention was focused on their baby boy, Chip.

I was given a choice of any room upstairs in the empty bunkhouse and allowed to use the cannery bicycle—a dreadfully heavy thing. I was told to keep it on cannery property.

Buildings were on pilings extending out over the water. Decking inside was dry and flat and safe, but one time, I went out on a part of the wharf that was attached to the shore. It was raining, and the bike's front wheel slipped on the wet planks when I attempted to circle back. The tide was out, and with no rail to prevent it, the bike went over the edge, and I landed face down on sharp rocks below.

It took some moments to regain myself. I then dragged the bike up the beach and onto the pier and stood in the rain, picking shards of shale out of my bleeding face and nose—pieces combined with blood and mud. I was never sure every piece was found and removed, but I guess it was, since nothing embedded has ever triggered airport security.

The bike was fine.

VILLAGE LIFE SLOWLY turned from 1951 to 1952, and by then, I had made friends with the untamable Arnold Joseph. Together, we thought up a game of pretending to be blind, and when Ralph Fenner, the school principal's son, arrived from the States during his summer break, he wanted to play too. The game went like this: One was to pretend to be blind—no cheating. He was to keep his eyes shut no matter what. The second player was to lead the blind, and no nasty tricks! Now having Ralph, we made up a third role, and that was to keep clear and not interfere.

We went about taking turns in the different roles on rocky beaches, along forest trails, over roots, boulders, and through underbrush. One day while playing the game—when Ralph was leading, Arnold was blind, and I was staying out of the way—we neared Arnold's house. He knew where he was but kept his eyes closed. Ralph guided him to the wooden walk that spanned the sea of mud that served as Arnold's front yard.

From there, Ralph began leading Arnold up the steps to the high porch. Arnold needed no coaching, but from my staying-out-of-the-way perspective, it seemed that Arnold's course up the steps was leading to the left, and there was no handrail. Just short of the porch, he stepped into air and fell over sideways, landing in the soupy mud.

He continued to lie there, half immersed in the muck, with his eyes still trustingly closed, when suddenly, we realized that Arnold's fearsome father was opening the door. Boys, you know, are boys: Ralph and I ran away.

I'm not sure one would classify such behavior as getting into serious trouble, but mostly for being young and silly and oblivious. One summer day, for example, we started wondering if we could drink upside down.

Good question. We had already tried kneeling at the side of a creek and found it *was* possible to suck up water, but our curiosity required being *truly* upside down, and we found the perfect place to test the question: from a solid limb jutting out from a big evergreen tree behind the newly constructed medical-clinic building.

There were a lot of big trees near that clinic; the forest had been cleared to make room for the place. I was never sure why it was me and not Arnold or Ralph that ended up being the upside-down one. My head was maybe five feet off the ground when hanging by the knees, and when Arnold went into the clinic and came back with a glass of water.

The first thing I noticed when attempting to drink was that the glass had to rest on the *upper lip,* but after a few tries, I got what you might say was the hang of it, and yes, it *is* possible to drink upside down.

I was still hanging there when Nurse Auntie Ev came bursting out of the clinic with a very stern look on her face, and said, "You boys are up to no good."

If she had just stopped there, there would have been no confusion. She was likely a good nurse but had three quirks: She had no sense of humor, knew nothing about twelve-year-old boys, and had the habit of tacking little words on the end of an otherwise good sentence. In this case, she added, "Are you not?"

Think about it. How would you answer this? "You boys are up to no good, are you not?"

I answered her straight: "Yes, we are not." And then I added, "No, I mean yes, we are not."

Her eyes narrowed, and her voice became rigid. "Don't get smart with me, young man!" I tried to explain what we were doing but her ears were closed to all reasoning. She demanded the glass back.

That was back in 1952. Even then, she was an old lady, around twenty-eight, I guess. Time moved on. She never married, never looked any different, and ended up in Bellingham, Washington, where she retired as the county nurse and died in 2007.

By then, my wife Rachel and I lived on Vancouver Island. I headed the work of Coastal Missions. Interestingly, in spite of that awkward, early upside-down misunderstanding, she became one of my life encouragers.

A memorial service was held at her church. I was up the coast and unable to be there but sent a message to be read. Some weeks later, Rachel and I, and others who were especially endeared, spread her ashes from the deck of the mission vessel *Coastal Messenger* as it circled in Stuart Channel a distance off the mission base at Chemainus.

Getting back to the subject of boys and Klawock, during the height of the salmon season, men were out on fish boats and cannery tenders, and everybody else who could work was busy at the fish plant. We younger boys played in and out of buildings, with our main responsibility being to keep out of the way.

There was no last-minute planning with cannery people. All things needed were brought by ship from Seattle. Flattened cans and lids made a formidable accumulation, and because of their weight, boxes were meticulously stacked in the warehouse. Corners were crisscrossed like brickwork.

A machine made flattened cans round and put their bottoms on. Women wearing oilcloth aprons loaded the cans with fish. Another machine put the lids on. Cans were then placed on iron trays and wheeled into giant cookers. The finished product was placed in case-lots and stacked, ready to be shipped.

Children in that part of the world easily accepted lower temperatures, cloudy skies, and rain, but when days of drizzle persisted as it did that summer, several of the boys found places to play inside the cannery warehouse. It came as a surprise one day when several of them asked me to come and see their secret place.

By then, the building was full enough to block most of the natural light from windows. I followed as they climbed upward on vertical structures and then swung from beam to beam over the tops of cardboard boxes. Brownish light from electric bulbs cast grotesque shadows. We dropped down onto the surface at a "staircase" of boxes, leading down to a cavern they had made by removing boxes and skillfully adding them to the great pile in the warehouse.

I received word a few days later, saying I was to go immediately to the cannery office. The big void had been discovered. Empty sections had seriously confused warehouse counts, and I was cited as the one who had done it. Charges were hastily dismissed, however, when my scrawny size was contrasted to the weight of boxes and the beefy arms of the boys who had laid the charge.

Mary Ellen Wilson

THIS CHAPTER MOVES ahead several years to a warm September day in 1958, when I stood in line with others registering for classes at Seattle Pacific College. Mary Ellen, a graceful, cultured young lady from Moose Jaw, Saskatchewan, was standing just ahead. She seemed surprised that I had never heard of Moose Jaw, Saskatchewan, but then I was surprised that she had never heard of Sitka, Alaska. Both of us were entering the prestigious music program at Seattle Pacific College.

I had always appreciated music; my parents and older siblings sang and played instruments. Being the youngest, I usually just listened. At age eleven, I purchased a harmonica at the local everything store in Klawock, but the precious little thing fell out of my shirt pocket and overboard a few days later, with one tiny splash and a few bubbles. It was a lesson never to forget about shirt pockets when you live on a ship. I went back and bought another one, but learning to play it was much more difficult than anticipated. I often practiced under the covers—something you can't do with most musical instruments.

My brother Frank played the trombone. One Sunday morning, he was playing in church. Children were climbing on, under, and around church pews, so little notice was given to the untamed curiosities of little Thurston Keta until he grabbed the trombone's slide and hung on. The music took a few strange wows, but Frank kept playing as he shook the little guy off.

I wanted to learn to play a brass instrument too; there were several different ones kept in *Gleaner*'s ammunition locker. When given permission to choose one, I picked a baritone horn—one that is held against the chest while blowing through the mouthpiece and fingering the notes like a trumpet. I brought it to my quarters, but of course, couldn't play it.

Gleaner was a busy hospital ship and no one was available to teach me, so noting the words "SELMER" and "Elkhart, Indiana" on the instrument's bell, I addressed an envelope with those very words (there were no postal codes in those days) and enclosed a penciled letter with a sketch of the instrument, asking for an instruction book. The letter went out on the freight boat, and from there, I more or less forgot about it, since mail to and from Prince of Wales in those days was subject to weather and often took weeks to get anywhere.

Sometime later, a packet arrived and was for me. Inside was an instruction book with black and white photos that looked just like the instrument. The cost of the book, one dollar, was clearly printed on its cover, but a note was enclosed saying, "No charge." It would have been interesting to know what the person in Indiana must have thought when receiving a child's penciled letter from Alaska.

Gleaner had watertight compartments and my quarters were in the forepart, with two steel bulkheads separating it from the rest of the ship. That arrangement must have been a blessing to others since my first tones attempting to learn the instrument could have passed for those of a distressed elephant.

I spent hours learning to play from the instruction book, and that learning contributed to learning music in another way. When in church, my father sang the bass line precisely as it was written in a hymnbook, and this happened at the time in my life when my voice was lowering into the bass-clef range. Noting my attempt to read the music, he used his little finger on the page to assist my following along. Between that prompting and his voice, and the sound of the baritone horn in my head, I learned to anticipate the sound of a note before hearing it.

Getting back to Mary Ellen, the following weekend was a Seattle Pacific College outing to Lincoln Park for new students. Mary Ellen was there, and it seemed urgent to her that I meet her roommate Rachel Smithwick, who was from Alaska.

When I questioned Rachel, she told me that, yes, her parents had been in Anchorage when she was born. They had made a few trips between Anchorage and Seattle by steamship, but she now lived in Washington. Her father was a cattle rancher living near Yakima.

Having pleasing brown skin, dark hair, and deep brown eyes, I asked if she was native to Alaska. "No," she explained, "I just stand in front of a window and tan."

Something came along some weeks into the school year that prompted me to ask Mary Ellen to accompany me. As soon as she got back to the dorm, Rachel asked if she'd had a good time. "Sure," Mary Ellen said, "we talked about you."

Speaking again about the college music program, I was given an opportunity to audition for the a cappella choir. A piece of music was thrust into my hand.

"Here, sing the baritone line," the lady said. The score was totally unfamiliar. She peeled off an introduction and looked at me expectantly.

Swallowing, I asked myself, *How'd I get into this?* Then I sucked in my breath and sang what was in my hands. She stopped abruptly, and with a ho-hum expression, said, "Fine." Then she called for the next student.

Being in the choir meant three hours of practice each week. I was to memorize the words and the baritone line of several pieces of music.

The following spring, the choir went on a musical tour—with a chartered bus and driver— into Oregon and places in Washington. Its driver readily learned every student's name and sat in on every concert.

That tour included visiting the State Capitol building in Olympia, Washington, where the choir began singing while standing on marble steps in the rotunda. The great dome above added a magnificent dimension to the sound. By then, the driver had memorized all the music and was happily singing with the tenors.

I was also in the college orchestra. By then, I could also play B-flat or E-flat tuba. Quite outside any school obligation, I was part of a six-person German band that played typical oom-pa-pa music from a book that included interrupting jokes, much like the two old geezers, Statler and Waldorf, on *The Muppet show.*

In the many happenings of college life, something came up that I'd never heard of: Sadie Hawkins Day, which was a spoof of sorts that came out of a comic book in the thirties. It was a day when female students asked male students for a date.

I was pleased when Rachel asked me to accompany her to breakfast in the cafeteria; I was attracted to her from the time I first laid eyes on her, when Mary Ellen had introduced us.

Our breakfast together was delightful, but barely what you'd call a date. I had the E-flat tuba and was committed to a morning oom-pa-pa performance with the German band.

Clap for Service

THE COLLEGE CAMPUS was only blocks away from the ship canal that connects to the sea, and I often went for walks there to clear my head, not caring if it was rainy or clear. I would stroll past the Foss shipyard and other waterfront interests and sometimes all the way to Fishermen's Terminal. There, I discovered an ex-navy subchaser, and at first opportunity took Rachel to see it. What better way to explain *Gleaner* than to show her a ship almost like it?

Owners Jim and Ruth Neely welcomed us. This was my real world, and Rachel admired me that way. I admired her too. It was only weeks later when I asked her to be my wife.

Sabre Craft Boat Company was close to the college and a place I found to be especially interesting. Big sliding doors were usually open during the workday, allowing me to watch the boat building taking place inside.

My first interest in boat carpentry came at age eleven, watching the powerful hands of ship's carpenter Sid King at work when *Gleaner* was being transformed into a hospital ship.

Even more interesting was a local man, Spencer Williams. He was a dark-faced, middle-aged native man who had a boat shop near *Gleaner*. His only power tool was a big band saw, powered by a slow-turning, two-flywheel gas engine. He did everything else by hand.

Spencer was a woodworking genius in my estimation. He had an exacting eye, able to judge lengths, size, depth, and angle, and besides that, he knew and used numerous boat-building techniques that simplified the layout of complex shapes. He had no objection to my watching and took time on occasion to explain exactly what he was doing.

I was standing looking in the big doors at Sabre Craft one day when the shop foreman, Lewis, a well-groomed and most courteous fellow, noted my interest, welcomed me into the shop, and showed me around. Apparently noting my comprehension, he said that they needed someone to work with the hull builder and urged me to consider the job. I explained that I was presently attending Seattle Pacific College and wouldn't be free until April.

He said he would hold the job open.

His offer was a thrill and relief. Attending college was delightful but had no foreseeable relation to real life and earning; I was anxious to get on with things.

The Sabre Craft foreman was good to his word and put me on the job when I finished the semester in April.

No longer in the college dorm, I took up couch residence at Marvin Milligan's place, a guy's hangout where no one knew how to cook or wash dishes. Somebody fried potatoes that tasted like fish.

Sabre Craft had a great team, but there was one mischievous fellow with a few accomplices working there too. He once cut plywood circles on a bandsaw, nailed them in a stack, and placed them on a paper plate. He then frosted it with rich, dark, creamy brown marine glue, making it look like a nice home-made cake. He put it out where Stew, the shop's strong man, would see it, and when he did, the fellow said it was Cleo's birthday (the lovely blonde woman in the office) and that the cake had been sent out for our enjoyment.

It was placed in the worker's lunchroom for afternoon break.

The break came, and the fellows gathered around. Stew was asked to cut it, and he started to. When realizing the joke was on him, he shrugged, turned away with a hurt look, and went back to work.

I took time off work at Sabre Craft to get married. The ceremony took place at Rachel's hometown church on June 27, 1959 (now more than sixty years ago). After an abbreviated honeymoon, we returned to Seattle and settled into a nice apartment on Argand Street, close to Sabre Craft so that I could easily walk to work.

Stew had gone through a painful divorce some months before, and the distress of it was written on his face each day at work.

It was some months after the cake thing when Rachel and I had him over to our place for supper. Happy conversation continued over cups of coffee into the evening. Noting that Stew's cup was empty, yet not wanting to interrupt our talking, I clapped my hands and pointed at Stew's cup. Rachel and I had recently seen that clap-for-service routine in the movie *The King and I*. Catching the cue, she quickly filled Stew's cup from the pot on the stove.

It happened a second time.

A few days later in the lunchroom, one of the guys began to tease me, saying that I must surely be a henpecked husband. Like crows, some of his cronies joined in. Seeing through their impish humor, I smiled and said nothing, which intensified their teasing even more.

They weren't noticing Stew's face. With each needling, his nostrils flared a little more, and suddenly, he raised a powerful fist, slammed it down on the table, and declared, "She's a GOOD woman! All he has to do is clap his hands and she does whatever he wants!" Nothing more was said.

As a P. S., that clap-your-hands-for-service thing never worked past that one evening.

Computer Printout

I CONTINUED WORK at Sabre Craft, and in time, our first son, Paul William, came along. Two years and two months later, our second son, James Allen, was born.

In the interest of expanding operations, Sabre Craft moved to Tacoma, and we rented a house in nearby Fife, next to Highway 99. You'd have thought ninety-nine was the speed limit. Traffic was relentless.

By then, we owned a hopped-up, pea-soup-green Ford coup that idled like a Harley. Getting out into the fast-moving stream of traffic took careful timing, but with that feisty little Ford, I'd rev the engine, pop the clutch, and catapult out like a jet off a carrier.

Tacoma Sabre Craft was a disappointment. Few of the Seattle guys moved with the company. The oversize building was poorly lit and always cold—too cold for glues to dry. Pneumatic power tools echoed through the place like screaming banshees. Unlike electric tools that warm the hands, those air-driven tools got colder as you used them.

There was none of the old team spirit.

My familiarity with jigs and templates, and having assisted Bud Stuart in the building of a few hundred boats by then, made me seem a threat to the new hull builder.

One of the incentives offered by the company to move to Tacoma was a raise in pay. That wasn't happening, and it was costing Rachel and I more to live there. I went to the office more than once, reminding of their promise.

One morning, I went in, gathered my tools, loaded them into the car, checked out at the office, returned home, changed clothes, and drove to Boeing's employment center in Renton.

The room was cheerfully lit and warm. Directions were simple: Fill out an application, submit it to the basket at the front, and be seated.

The room was full of hopefuls.

Someone in my past had advised me, "When you fill out a job application, be sure to include *every* machine you've ever operated, and *everything* you've ever done that relates to the work you are applying for." It took time, but the application was eventually placed in the basket.

Having used extra sheets, I was able to note when it was lifted out.

A man stood reading down its pages, and then, after considerable time, called upon two associates. I could see them discussing the information on the pages, and in time, I was called to the counter and asked to come around behind it, where I was introduced to a Mr. Leahy, who was a serious-looking man wearing a dark suit under a somber overcoat—obviously, someone of importance. After a brief exchange of words, I accompanied him to the nearby factory building, where he led the way to an elevator that emerged onto a windowed mezzanine floor, high above an extensive aircraft-assembly area.

I listened closely to everything he said and answered his questions carefully, while watching manned cranes sashaying back and forth high above the various stages of aircraft constructions taking place below.

When back in the employment office, I was told I was hired "as soon as the job is created." I returned home, wondering what those last words meant.

The phone rang a few days later. I was told to go to that same area on the mezzanine. Two others were there when I entered the room. They also wondered what our job assignment might be.

A man eventually stepped into the room and began explaining that our work would involve tooling and computerizations.

I soon realized that "tooling" did NOT mean screwdrivers, pliers, electric drills, or anything like that. Rather, it referred to things used to make airplane parts, starting with engineered drawings (blueprints). Templates, trim jigs, and such were tools, and it took several tools to make each airplane part.

A huge computer printout was given to each of us, listing airplane parts by number. The tools just spoken of had the same number, but like computer files, each had a different three-letter extension.

Information on the massive printout showed the start and finish dates for everything. The whole idea was to have an allotted number of parts ready on the shelf on the date stated. The printout identified what was behind schedule. Our newly created job was to investigate why something was behind schedule and use whatever it took to get it back on schedule.

Whoa, I said to myself, *just learning the different buildings and locations where things are done will take time.* And it did.

An office was set up in that same area with desks, filing cabinets, and telephones. A secretary was assigned even before we needed one. Tags were issued and to be worn on the lapel, allowing entry into the different areas in the plant.

Just getting started was a challenge, as we had no one to ask for help. Renton Boeing was in the infancy of computerizations. People knew little about computers in the early 1960s, beyond the fact that they could handle numbers faster and store information better than humans.

Those in authority were learners too.

Boeing's one big computer was like the control room of a large ship: excessively warm. This was back in the days of vacuum tubes. Everything was big. Gratings around the mainframe were elevated above the floor, with heaps of electrical cables strewn around underneath them linking the various components.

The printout worked well once we understood how to use it. An asterisk marked the number and extension of whatever was behind schedule, and highest priority was on whatever was the most behind. Each behind-schedule matter was handled as a separate investigation, which meant going to the area and dealing directly with the ones having the problem. Everything about an investigation was meticulously recorded and kept on file until the problem was resolved.

The job also required going to night school to learn how to read engineering drawings of every kind in the English language. I also took classes relating to tool and production planning, given by a gracious man, Walter Beard, who had authority to pull me from my regular work and usher me through different parts of the aircraft plant. He pointed out various manufacturing processes and introduced me to key persons. I kept careful notes and eventually made a handbook containing such information.

Walter gave particular attention to the mockup area. We watched the many craftsmen at work. At some point, he said, "We like boat builders." Pointing up at an electrical box nested in a massive mock wing, he said, "Hand one of those guys a piece of equipment to be installed in an airplane, and he'll make a replica from wood, mount it in place, and wire it in with a piece of hose, or wire, or whatever." He continued, "From there, the engineering people come around and copy the installation to their drawing."

Walter was in the process of writing a textbook on the subject he was teaching. He found my questions and observations helpful, and in the final, asked me to provide cartoon-like illustrations for its otherwise dry content.

The computer printout, as said earlier, made it easy to identify what was behind schedule. Finding a solution could be as simple as supplying a missing measurement. Other times, it was necessary to get design engineers together with the ones having trouble on the shop floor. When a problem was resolved, an immediate go-ahead was authorized by an ACDN—an 8 ½ by 11 piece of paper that also prompted behind-the-scene changes to prevent the problem occurring again.

On one occasion, I went to see about some matter having to do with planning. Paperwork was waiting for a three-digit number. The person who usually filled out the form had been absent from work for several days. Desiring to expedite the thing, I asked the supervisor what the number was for.

"I don't know," he said.

"Where does it come from?" I asked.

"From this book," he replied, as he pointed to a blue cover.

Paperwork at Boeing was a concern. Four point something pounds of paper were used for every pound of airplane that rolled out factory doors. In this case, the three-digit number, repeating 001 through 999, was found to be something used during World War II and was no longer needed for anything. In the long of it, the form was redesigned, not having space for it.

More persons were added to our team and a considerably larger office space was provided. It was there that I received some unique tutoring from an older gentleman who would often shuffle in and ask, "Got any coffee?"

He'd had a stroke and was supposed to stay away from coffee. He was, or had been, some kind of plant manager and seemed compelled to talk. I'd invite him to sit in my chair, pour him some coffee, pull up a stool, and listen as he spoke from long experience—one sentence might span decades.

Only later did it occur how much was gained by his personalized tutoring, but I am now so ashamed of my selfishness that it brings me to tears. I never thought to ask his last name.

The Off-Ramp

MANY THINGS CAME as a surprise when dealing with people at Boeing. Employees could be very different than they seemed. Things can seriously bog down in the hands of someone who loves work; what you actually need is good *completers*. One seemingly doing the least might be the most efficient. Lazy people can be the most enterprising when it comes to finding the easiest ways to get a job done.

Part of my job was to be ever watchful for inefficiencies. Lost seconds go unnoticed yet add up to minutes, and minutes add up to hours, and wasted hours mean wasted dollars. Repetitious jobs are best accomplished by choreographed teamwork. People not able to function in that environment needed to be elsewhere. In view of the many personalities and incredible labor that goes into building airplanes, it is understandable that manufacturers moved toward the use of programmable robotics as it became possible.

As more employees were added to our team, a second shift was advised, and I was asked to lead the way. In that transition, I somehow inherited a room full of female keypunch operators. That was an eye opener! Imagine me in charge of a room full of lipstick and painted fingernails. Fortunately, their direct supervisor was a mature woman able to control things, and I kept clear of the place except as called upon, usually because one of the girls was in a snit about something and refused to sit next to another. I'd attempt to hear the problem through (note that I said "attempt") and then move desks and connecting cables or whatever it took to make everyone happy.

Scott, a cheerful-faced fellow and always well dressed, remained on dayshift and became my counterpart. Shift change was at three-thirty. As the hands on the clock reached that time, Scott would stand up and politely hold the chair for me to sit. Such a changing of the guard was repeated time and again.

Rachel was by then serving as secretary for the 727 Hydraulics Engineering group in a different building, and they got off work at four forty-five. Such starting and quitting times for the different parts of the plant were staggered to minimize parking lot and highway congestion.

At three-thirty, the phone on my desk would ring. Scott knew it would be Rachel. Since clocks in the plant were not exactly synchronized, her call would sometimes come early. Scott would simply hand the phone to me.

One day, in mischievous humor, he picked up the phone and *didn't* hand it to me. Instead, he said, "Roy *was* here, but he walked out to the parking lot with his wife, you know, the tall good-looking woman in the IBM room."

Rachel, with quick wit, answered, "When he gets back, tell him his girl-friend called."

He then handed the phone to me.

Scott was a character. One day, the two of us and some others were seated around a huge boardroom table. A speaker lectured from oversize pages on a flipchart. Scott fought to keep his eyes open. He cradled his chin in his right palm and fell asleep in that position. The lecturer droned on. Scott's elbow began to slide toward the edge of the table, but the very moment it slipped off, his hand shot up as if hailing a cab. "I have a question," he said.

The fellow gave him permission to speak. Scott, in a most composed and intelligent manner, asked for clarification on a particular point.

The whole factory had character. Nobody left before quitting time, but the moment the bell rang, they stampeded. They could empty a parking lot like flushing a toilet. But, boy, those people were good drivers. You seldom heard of an accident. It helped, of course, to drive something that didn't matter if it was bumped. Back then, cars were built heavy and used leaded gasoline. Cold engines ran stinky enough to make one's eyes water. But who cared? The problem with social security back then was getting old enough to use it. At least half of everybody smoked and nobody expected to live much beyond seventy.

By then we owned a nice car—a green Studebaker—quiet—very unlike the jazzy little Ford, and lived on a quiet street where speed was not necessary.

One day, after parking along with others doing the same, I took my lunch and started toward the massive factory building. Elevated briefly near the security gates, I looked out over a sea of bobbing heads, trailing off toward the little square hole that served as the entrance into the great wall of the building. The sight of it caused a troubling feeling that was hard to describe and even harder to shake. Where had my *real* life gone?

Sometime after that, I had an appointment to keep in Seattle. All lanes bogged down to a crawl approaching the Mercer Island Bridge, and all hope of getting there on time died. Traffic inched forward, and I eventually got to an off-ramp, so I turned off and drove to a little café and parked.

After phoning ahead to explain the missed appointment, I sat at a table and sipped coffee from a white porcelain mug, while absently poking pieces of dry pastry into my mouth, feeling that something was deeply wrong. It wasn't merely the matter of traffic or missing an appointment but something deeper. Everything was so right ... yet so wrong.

Rachel and I were able to take special days together nearing Christmas. Her parents looked after our boys while we flew to Alaska to be with my side of the family. Sitka was stunningly beautiful under cold, crystal-clear skies. Our time was like a honeymoon. Family and friends pleaded with us to return and live there.

My brother Frank and his family had recently moved out of their cabin on Morne Island and into a house at Jamestown Bay, leaving the cabin vacant and free for our use. Frank was part owner of Tri-Ways Marina and said that they needed a person who could repair boats. The job was there and open for me. It was tempting, of course, but I felt an obligation to Boeing. My job paid well and had provided what amounted to a hands-on engineering education. I couldn't just walk away.

The time came to return to Seattle.

The aircraft spiraled down through dark, rain-filled clouds. Seattle could be seen under a layer of dark gray/brown smog. The sight of it caused that same repulsion to well up again, and everything suddenly made sense. I turned to Rachel and said, "Let's go back to Sitka."

Kapok Pillows

MOVING TO ALASKA would require serious planning. We'd need a boat big enough to carry our belongings from Seattle, yet small enough to be our daily transportation when living on Morne Island.

I searched over the next weeks and found a well-built twenty-seven-foot-long former Columbia River gillnet fish boat in La Conner, and phoned the number on the FOR SALE sign. The owner arrived in minutes. After an hour and a half assessment, we settled on a price.

He agreed to run the boat to Seattle, and a few days later, I met him at the locks when he arrived as planned. After securing at a nearby marina, I wrote out a check for the full amount and drove him back to his home.

The boat had never had an official name. Since it was made to handle fish-nets over the bow, we simply called it *The Bowpicker*.

By then, it was mid-January 1963, and weather was cold but also sunny and dry. The boat was hauled out of the water, and its bottom was cleaned and painted, and then after launching, I moved it to Fisherman's Terminal.

Still working second shift at Boeing in Renton, I used every possible opportunity to ready for the trip to Alaska. The boat's cabin top was repaired, combings around the forward hold were modified to receive hatch covers, an oil stove and tank was installed, a bright new galvanized garbage can was purchased to serve as a water barrel, as well as two enameled basins—one for washing dishes and the other for bathing and shaving.

Rachel and I gave notice at Boeing with the plan of wrapping up work in late March.

My friend, Bob Welfelt, was due for a furlough from the army that nicely coincided with my plans for making the voyage. Rachel and the boys would join her parents on April 3 and fly to Sitka on the fourteenth; Bob and I would leave Seattle on April 4 and get to Sitka when we could.

Bob arrived some hours before Rachel's parents appeared to pick up her and the boys, and the two of us waved goodbye as they all drove off.

The apartment had been emptied of everything except a huge pile of things needing to be packed and carried to *The Bowpicker*. I had collected burlap bags for that purpose. Trip after trip was made between the apartment and the boat over the next hours, and when loading was complete, hatch covers were put in place and a canvas tarp carefully battened over the top. A small wooden rowboat, which I'd purchased from a commercial fisherman days before, was placed upside-down on the canvas and lashed in place. A duffel bag containing my diving gear was pushed into a space under the deck at the stern.

We still needed to shop for groceries and deliver the green Studebaker to a car dealership in Ballard. Arrangement for the car had been made the week before, so after shopping, we drove to the dealership and completed the transaction. An employee then drove our groceries and us to *The Bowpicker* at Fishermen's Terminal.

When the car drove off, I stood watching in its direction for a long time. Mine was a most unusual feeling. All ties to Seattle had now been broken. Everything was now down to *The Bowpicker* and Bob and me ... and Sitka was a mighty long way away.

Boy, we were tired!

I was to sleep on the plywood platform beside the engine, and Bob on floorboards under the plywood. Clothing was strewn all over inside the postage-stamp-size cabin, along with cooking utensils, navigation stuff, sleeping bags, and the groceries that needed to be put ... *somewhere*.

We eventually crawled into sleeping bags, too tired to think about tomorrow's departure, and too tired to care about having only our coats as mattresses. Kapok lifejackets served as pillows.

The air was cold and damp the next morning, and getting organized took time. It was mid-morning when we untied and motored to the fuel dock to top off *The Bowpicker's* gas tank and fill the jerrycans beside the cabin. When finished, we left Fishermen's Terminal and went out through the locks.

The wind and seas were from the southeast. Beyond the fairway buoy, the stern rose on a sizable wave and abruptly dropped into the following trough. It was only then that the gravity of the moment fully dawned: We were finally on our way to Alaska.

That was April 4, 1963.

Memories Teenage Years

THIS CHAPTER MOSTLY recounts memories of Bob and me talking from sleeping bags that first night after leaving Seattle.

I first met Bob in the summer of 1955 after I joined *Gleaner* at Mount Edgecombe (Sitka) after grade 10 in California. I knew no one except my parents in that part of Alaska. Some weeks later, they and several others were at a picnic gathering at Halibut Point when bright-eyed, fourteen-year-old Peggy Burnham befriended me.

She spoke enthusiastically about Bob Welfelt, saying he was in Billings, Montana at a baseball camp and insisted that he and I would make great friends. I met Bob a few days later, and she was right.

That September, Bob and I attended Sitka High. We rode the passenger ferry, locally known as the "shore boat" from the Mount Edgecombe side of the channel to the Sitka side. Once on the Sitka side, we walked and ran the distance to school.

Over the following years, Bob and I hiked trails, climbed mountains, played in open boats, and did most everything together.

The Russians left many cannons behind when Alaska was sold to the U.S. in 1867. That winter, during a particularly cold stretch, Bob noticed a cannon ball down in the throat of one. Muck and moisture freezing in behind the ball had slowly pushed it upward. We figured we could hurry the process by pouring a bit of water down the cannon barrel each morning on our way to school.

It worked. The cannon ball was eventually sticking halfway out of the barrel. Other boys tried to knock it out with a stick, but it was Bob who rightfully managed to free what turned out to be an eleven-pound rusty sphere of Russian history. He took it home and added it to his mother's collection of rarities.

In 1956, we learned that the Territory of Alaska was making land parcels available through something called the Homesite Act, and from what we heard, the claim had to be less than five acres, and a cabin had to be built with at least one door and one window.

Bob and I, both age sixteen, and being much more sound in body than in mental maturity, went to work not bothering to pursue details of the Act.

A big shipping crate had been left on the long wharf a distance from *Gleaner*. With youthful brawn and teenage brains, we managed to scoot the thing to the edge, and with the help of the dock crane, we lowered it into the sea. Using skiff and outboard motor, it was towed the long mile to uninhabited Morne Island. Using leverage and brute force, we were able to slide it a safe distance in from the rocky beach and place it on a log foundation.

Over the next weeks, the box was given a pitched roof using galvanized roofing we'd gotten from a crew that was demolishing an airplane hangar on Japonski Island—one of many structures left over from the war.

Bob and I lost track of time one day while engaged in the cabin project; we were in desperate need of something to eat. Survival stuff carried in the skiff was down to just one can of sausage meat—again, something left over from the war. With starvation as in our case, people will eat most anything. The can was opened with the axe, and fatty chunks were placed on the back of a shovel and fried over the campfire.

The cabin was eventually completed with a door, window, small porch, and a chair from someplace. Two bunk surfaces were built into the back wall. There was no stove, no heat, no bathroom, no sink, no carpet, no key, no landlord, no rent, no taxes, and no water—except for rain, Morne Island had no water.

There was a metal sign on the crate, which was now part of the outer wall, that said something in a foreign language. When our friend Henry Langfeldt came to see the cabin, he laughed at the German words, which meant, "For local freight only."

Our application for owning the island was denied, because we were not yet eighteen, but my brother Frank took over and did everything that met the demands of the Homesite Act.

He, Nancy, and their family lived there for several years.

Bob and I were soon off to other adventures. This time it was mountain climbing, specifically Bear Mountain above Silver Bay—more than four thousand feet right up from the sea. Every precaution was taken for this one. We roped ourselves with a seventy-foot-long tether and climbed the snowy peak a distance apart, just in case one or the other slipped off or fell into a crevice. The mountain ridge was sharp. Wind had stacked ice and snow on one side and scoured the other side almost bare.

When at the very peak, still a distance apart and joined by a tether, we loosed some fractured sheets of slate and wrestled them around into position to use as sleds to slide down the snowy side of the mountain. It was extremely steep at the top, but less so at the lower elevation. It was reasoned that sledding down would make our descent much easier.

I positioned myself on my rock sled with heels firmly planted to prevent the perhaps one hundred-pound rock from sliding. Bob, poised thirty or forty feet off to my left, was doing the same with his rock. The plan was that I would release my sled first and then Bob would release his, before the rope became tight.

The safety rope was carefully laid out between us so that nothing could go wrong.

Again, we rehearsed the plan: When sliding down the slope, when it seemed we were down the mountain far enough, I would dig my heels in, raise up enough to let my rock go, and bring myself to a stop. Bob's part was to do the same.

Sitting on my rock, teetering on the ridge and holding back with both heels, I turned to Bob and said, "Ready?"

"Ready," he answered.

Again, I said, "Ready?"

He again repeated, "Ready."

With that, I let go and took off at a speed of ... well ... whatever speed a big flat rock goes down a seventy percent incline on an icy snowfield, with my eyes watering and mouth and cheeks bulged out in the wind. Talk about exhilarating! And a quick loss of altitude.

I began to dig my heels in at around the fifteen-hundred-foot level, rose up enough to let my rock sled go, and brought myself to a stop while shouting, "Perfect!"

I turned to Bob to share the most exiting ride of a lifetime. He was staggering around looking confused and pulling snow out of his pockets.

"What are you doing?" I asked.

"I couldn't get my rock started," he said.

When Bob saw the rope coming tight and realized his rock was stuck, he had gotten up and tried to run. Being unable to run fast enough, he was dragged and spun around, doing cartwheels at high speed until things were brought to a stop.

Our next adventure (or more accurately "innovation") was a water chair. You know, a chair on water skis. No one to my knowledge had ever thought of such a thing. The idea was that the water chair would slide along nicely at the end of a towrope behind Bob's outboard-powered skiff. It was assumed that the chair could be steered by leaning left or right.

Construction took place on the wharf beside *Gleaner*. The Coast Guard Buoy Tender *Sorrel* was tied there. Many of its crew was aroused to curiosity. They asked us to make a run past their ship when the ski chair was up and running.

First testing took place a mile out of town at a perfect launch pad: a slippery, slimy, low-in-the-water log sticking out the end of a float. The empty chair was placed on the log, with skis straddling each side of it. The towline from the skiff was attached and brought up tight. With throttle, the chair slid to the end of the log, came up on its skis, and followed the boat beautifully. Next, a big rock was added to it. Again, all worked perfectly. When the boat slowed down, the chair leaned over and the rock fell off. Finally, it was time for the human test. Bob ran the skiff, and I assumed the administrative position: I took the chair.

The line was attached as before but with a quick-release knot, which could easily be let go by a jerk. Did I really say "jerk?"

The outboard motor roared to life and the chair came up on its skis with me on it. I had to clamp my knees together to keep water from spraying up in my face.

Plans were to run toward Sitka and past the Coast Guard ship then circle back to the airplane float. I'd let the tow rope go at just the right time, steer for the inclined section of the float, slide up on it, come to a stop, stand up, and be the first in the world to have ridden a ski chair.

Low groundswells were feeding in from the Pacific as we rounded into Middle Channel. The boat sped down the face of the first swell and slowed as the boat began to climb the back of the next. With loss of speed, the ski tips started to dig in. I leaned back in the chair and recovered the situation. It happened three or four times, and by then, I realized the chair should have been mounted a bit farther back on the skis. I also noted that leaning side to side did not steer the chair and wondered how I was going to land it at the airplane float. This, of course, was before wetsuits, and the seawater temperature around Sitka was low on the Fahrenheit scale.

The Coast Guard guys were on deck and waved enthusiastically as we passed. We continued speeding along the surface at full throttle. It was one of those lovely days when dozens of people were out enjoying the sun on the end of the cold storage pier. Many were waving; some were cheering.

The ferry was just then making its way across the channel. That was no concern, but the sharp waves it was creating was problematic. We hit the bow wave, and the skis dug in. I leaned back. The next wave hit, and I leaned back again. Then the third wave hit, and I leaned way back, but this time the back of the chair let go. The back of my head hit the water first, then my feet.

In an instant, I was plunged deep beneath the surface, looking up at floating wreckage.

End of water chair 1956.

Such were the many memories that Bob and I shared from our sleeping bags in the tiny cabin of *The Bowpicker* that first night out of Seattle.

It was getting late. The little oil stove murmured softly. I reached over and shut it off. A little round hole in its iron lid allowed light from the dying flame to dance on the ceiling.

Off and Beyond

THE NEXT MORNING, still wrapped in the sleeping bag, I reached out, started the fire, and put the teakettle on.

The cabin was beginning to warm as I stood and dressed, started the engine, and stepped outside to give Bob room to get out of his sleeping bag and get dressed.

The Bowpicker was operated from a raised surface behind its cabin, a structure that broke the wind but gave no relief from the morning's chill. My teeth were chattering when Bob handed me a porcelain mug of hot steaming coffee; I held it to my chest trying to absorb its heat.

We went into Port Townsend and contacted a marine mechanic after noting that the engine was inclined to overheat. I wondered if it was because *The Bowpicker* was now carrying the added weight of its cargo. The mechanic arrived and quickly found the problem: a worn-out cooling pump, which he easily replaced. We were then on our way again.

The late afternoon air chilled dramatically as Point Wilson slowly faded into the haze astern.

Accurate navigation is important in this area; currents are swift. The compass was placed at the steering station as the sun went down. We continued in what soon became a surrealistic world of mist and darkness. I was relieved when the lighted buoy off Salmon Bank came into view, and minutes later, the shape of Whale Rocks could be seen by the low illumination of *The Bowpicker*'s navigation lights.

We continued in San Juan Channel and tied to a float at Friday Harbor.

Tired and chilled, we set off with towels, hoping the port facility had a public shower. It did: the first coin-operated one Bob and I had ever seen. Bob insisted that I go first, so fully in the skinny, I inserted the needed quarter and twisted the dial.

Oh, the blessed refreshment of that hot shower!

I continued to luxuriate, wondering how long a quarter would last, when there was a metallic click and the stream suddenly turned ice cold.

THE ALARM CLOCK sounded before 5:00 a.m. on the third day of our trip. I reached from my sleeping bag and lit the stove. Once satisfied that it was burning, I snuggled down again until the teakettle began to whistle. By then, the cabin was warm.

When dressed, I started the engine, went out, untied, and we were off. Bob soon had coffee in my hands and then began preparing breakfast, a routine that worked well—so well, in fact, that we choreographed ourselves in that manner for the rest of the trip.

We took turns steering through lovely island passages where red and gold trunks of Arbutus trees mingle with darker evergreens and continued through Dodd Narrows and on to Nanaimo. After clearing Customs and topping the gas tank, we secured *The Bowpicker* in the inner basin and took a walk ashore.

Fragrances, reminders of spring, filled the air.

Coming upon a café bustling with patrons, we went in and were soon seated. Noting the modest prices, we ordered steak dinners. Our presence somehow aroused curiosities, especially when people learned we were on our way to Alaska.

I carried the tab to the cashier, a burly fellow wearing a stained apron reminiscent of a butcher's. He took the bill and without explanation drew a line through the total, halving the amount. Perhaps it was his way of saying, "Welcome to Nanaimo," or "Good luck on your trip." Maybe both. Something about his face seemed to say, "Don't ask."

We left early the next morning. A light southeasterly wind gave a boost up the Strait of Georgia, and in time, became more forceful. Seas reacting against an opposing current created massive breaking rips when nearing Cape Mudge. *The Bowpicker* was thrown about wildly.

The current had turned favorable by the time we reached Seymour Narrows.

Hours later, we went in and tied to some floating equipment and had supper at a place shown on the navigation chart as Rock Bay. It had been a long day—one hundred nautical miles at about seven knots.

By then it was raining.

A logger appeared out of the darkness as dishes were being washed, but because he was wearing caulk boots, he declined stepping on board. After a short conversation, he rolled a gas drum to the stern of *The Bowpicker* and announced that he was ready to fill the boat's tank. "Free gas," he said. "The little you guys need is less than what we *spill* around here every day." Then, as suddenly as he had appeared, he was gone.

"A gas angel," I jokingly suggested, "wearing caulk boots."

It continued to rain. I removed the lid from the shiny new garbage can that served as a water barrel.

It was full and overflowing in the morning when we left. Alert Bay was more than eight hours away. Rain persisted, wind increased, and seas grew steeper, keeping pace as we progressed westward in Johnstone Strait.

Flags of laundry were flying from clotheslines as *The Bowpicker* rounded Cormorant Island into Alert Bay.

I took this one picture of Bob as we stretched our legs ashore. We didn't want to take too long, as it was another twenty-six nautical miles to Port Hardy.

We moved to the fuel float, topped the tank, and were again on our way. By then, the sky had cleared and the wind had switched to westerly—a wind that dramatically increased after passing Pultney Point.

A steel crabber not far ahead sent sheets of spray high into the air each time its blunt nose smashed into a wave. Two salmon trollers took up position like ducks in a row behind us, rising and falling dramatically in the steep seas.

I was outside operating *The Bowpicker* while Bob was inside trying to stop an annoying drip coming in from a crack in one window. We traded places after a time, which put Bob outside facing the fast-flying spray, and me in the shelter of the cabin.

Looking back through the cabin's open door, I watched as the nearest of the two trollers rose high on a great curling crest—much of its keel exposed for a moment—before plunging deep into the following trough.

Minutes later, both trollers turned back.

The wind increased and our progress was slowed, our visibility restricted by continuous spray and failing daylight. The heavy crabber continued to smash determinedly westward. We eventually rounded into the protection of Hardy Bay and headed toward the only visible wharf.

When close, the headlights of a vehicle emerged out of somewhere and bobbed along planks to the end of the pier. A man climbed out and shouted down, giving directions for entering the protected inner harbor. Following his welcoming prompt, we went in and tied to a float and stopped the engine. By then, everything was dark, silent, and calm.

Marine Atlas Volume Two

DEPARTURE FROM PORT Hardy was before daybreak. Luckily the wind had blown itself out during the night.

Having completed *Marine Atlas Volume One*, I now opened volume two and assessed our progress. *The Bowpicker* had traveled about three hundred nautical miles in five days, perhaps a third of the distance to Sitka.

The swells were gentle as we rounded Pine Island into Queen Charlotte Sound. *The Bowpicker* was brought to a stop long enough to launch the rowboat. I got in with the camera and shoved off. Bob maneuvered the craft some distance, then made a high-throttled pass. I pressed the shutter, then quickly sat down, hoping its sharp bow wave wouldn't swamp the tiny boat.

It was dark when *The Bowpicker* reached Bella Bella. Streaks of light from houses reflected across the water, making entrance into the little harbour confusing.

Once in, we secured to a float for the night. Supper had been eaten hours earlier and the stove was off, but Bob lit it again to heat water for hot chocolate—canned milk, chocolate powder, and hot water.

I dug out my Sony portable radio and searched the short-wave frequencies for news. Amid electronic squeals and squawks, I heard, "Nuclear submarine *Thresher* ... thirty miles off Portsmouth ... exceeded depth ... persons lost." It was difficult to piece the story together at the time. The nuclear submarine *Thresher* had just come out of the shipyard at Portsmouth, New Hampshire, to undergo tests at sea, with about thirty persons in addition to her crew of nearly one hundred. The rescue vessel *Skylark* accompanied her.

Thresher submerged about thirty miles off the coast while *Skylark* kept in contact. At one point during deepwater tests, a voice from the submarine reported, "Experiencing minor problem," followed by the sound of gushing air. Then, after a period of silence, came the garbled words, "Exceeding test depth."

I slept fitfully, vividly imagining the sound of wrenching steel and thoughts of spiraling fearfully downward into the inky abyss and crashing onto the sea floor.

We left early the next morning and soon encountered fog. The deep-throated voice of the foghorn at Ivory Island was blasting out its signal at regular intervals as we passed. Milbanke Sound was calm except for low groundswells marching in from the southwest. By then, everything was enshrouded in a ghostly blanket of gray.

Navigation was by reckoning. When figures indicated we *should* be at the buoy marking Vancouver Rock, and we could see nothing, the engine was brought to an idle. It was hard to know what to do; suddenly, there was a brief opening of glorious sunlight just enough to see the buoy off to the right. With renewed confidence, the throttle was brought up to speed and *The Bowpicker* again entered dense fog as happy porpoises arrived to play at the bow.

In time, the fog dissipated but the chill remained.

The voyage continued past Klemtu and northward in Tolmie Channel, the start of a series of waterways that well describes "the Inside Passage." The ruins of a wharf, deserted buildings, and a tall brick stack could be seen as we passed the mouth of Swanson Bay.

An hour and a half later, we came upon a hand-painted sign attached to a tree: "GAS." We soon reached Butedale. A man came down to the fuel barge to attend the pump.

When we finished filling, *The Bowpicker* was moved to a nearby float beside a great forest of pilings. From there, we climbed the steep ramp to the wharf and store, where we spoke to a lady behind the counter. She suggested we hike to the lake and dam.

We did, and after a time, started down. A continuous whirring sound could be heard coming from the powerhouse. I looked inside and watched two sizable turbines rotating unhurriedly, while thinking to myself, *A thousand years from now, these turbines will still be turning out endless electricity.*

After paying for the gas and purchasing a few items at the store, including a big can of Empress brand apricot jam, we were on our way, and three hours later, were in Wright Sound. There, looking to the south (and to my utter astonishment), we saw a ship's lifeboat with people in it, but for whatever reason, they were neither rowing nor waving. I turned *The Bowpicker* in that direction and called Bob. As we got closer, it was possible to see that they were all wearing typical heavy-rubber rain gear with Sou'wester rain hats. The engine was slowed as we prepared to come alongside.

Only when yards away did it become evident that shapes and sizes were being stretched by a strange prismatic effect of the atmosphere, or perhaps due to an hallucinatory reaction to eating too much apricot jam. In any case, these were not men in a lifeboat but cormorants on a sun-bleached log. Sheepishly, I brought the bow of *The Bowpicker* around and resumed in the direction of Grenville Channel.

We continued to a tiny wooded islet in an indentation along the shore just below Sainty Point. I eased *The Bowpicker* up close to a rock outcropping where Bob got off and secured a long line to a tree. When he was back on board, I backed the craft away and lowered the anchor over the stern.

It was soon dark. Ours had been a good run—one hundred nautical miles from Bella Bella.

The fog that morning seemed *days* ago.

It was amazing how handy Bob was with food. After peeling, boiling, and cubing potatoes, he cut and fried them with pieces of bacon and little squares of canned spam. He served this with canned tomatoes, sauerkraut, and canned sweet brown bread.

He had an interesting way of preparing the bread. He removed the label and lowered the can into boiling water. After some minutes, he lifted it out and used the can opener to open both ends. Pushing the bread out little by little from one end, he used a knife and the rim of the can as a guide to cut thin slices, which were then eaten with melted butter dripping off our fingers.

Anchoring with a line to a tree worked well. The downside was that Bob had to be up and outside the next morning to let the line go from the tree.

Several chilly hours after running the distance of Grenville Channel, we emerged into the open area past Morning Reef, where the sun began to warm. Wavelets from a freshening breeze turned the sea into a sparkle of endless diamonds.

The skies began filling with white tails, and by mid-afternoon, it was fully overcast. The morning breeze had by then turned into broad sweeping seas as *The Bowpicker* pitched and rolled its way to Prince Rupert.

It was past business hours when we arrived at the fuel dock. The attendant kindly opened valves and served us anyway. After moving and securing to a nearby float, we climbed a gangway that led to street level. Having spent the past days closely associated with the disciplines of the voyage, it seemed strange to be in the midst of people walking, talking, and laughing in a well-lit city. Realizing our bedraggled appearance, we returned to the boat—by then it was completely dark—and using a flashlight, we loosed lashings to the hold and pulled the canvas back enough to gain access to a bag with clean clothes. Tall pilings and darkness provided ample privacy to change on the hatch cover.

Ashore again, we walked and gawked curiously into storefronts, until the tantalizing aromas from a Chinese restaurant had us seated at a table. Being aware of our tiredness after eating, we returned to *The Bowpicker* and went right to bed.

Murder Cove

WE LEFT PRINCE Rupert by way of the Venn Passage before the light of morning. Having only *Marine Atlas Volume Two* as a guide and not a proper chart, navigation was confusing.

Wind feeding from a northeast direction intensified in Chatham Sound, resulting in conditions too great to turn around. Our only choice was to pray, hang on, and keep the bow to the wind with reduced throttle.

To my horror, the engine began to stutter. I feared that, if it should quit, *The Bowpicker* would turn sidewise, allowing seas to fill the stern cockpit.

We continued to limp forward at a greatly reduced rate. After perhaps two hours, and with great relief, we were able to enter into the shelter of a little channel between Kanagunut and Sitklan Islands.

At some point, we had crossed the invisible line into Alaska.

Ours was a protected spot but far from any place of help for engine trouble. Bob was not mechanically minded, and so the weight of finding and fixing the problem lay solely on me.

Perhaps the severe motion of *The Bowpicker* had stirred up sediment in the gas tank. When examined, the filter *was* found to be dirty, and I sensed some relief, but after cleaning it, the engine still ran very poorly—a situation that left me feeling ill with concern.

We dared not continue with a sick engine; we still had Dixon Entrance to cross.

Our selection of mechanical tools was limited, and for that reason, I was hesitant to start taking things apart, but what choice was there? With great care, I removed the carburetor and began carefully disassembling and cleaning every component. There would be no help if a part was lost or damaged.

In time, when fully assembled, mounted, and tried, the engine started easily (to our greatest relief) and ran properly, so we hauled anchor and left, but the storm was still raging, so we retreated to the same haven and once again dropped the anchor.

Maybe it was impatience and wishful thinking that convinced us, some hours later, to pull the anchor and leave a second time. The wind feeding out of Portland Inlet had eased, but as we continued on and into Dixon Entrance, massive breaking seas again threatened. With relief, we were able to get safely into the protection of Foggy Bay and into a tiny spot out of all wind *and* wave. The anchor was lowered to the bottom a third time that dreadful day.

It was a low point for me. Rachel and our boys were on my mind, as this was the day they were to fly from Seattle. I hoped her trip would not be difficult. Those little guys were energetic. Paul had just turned three, and Jim was ten months. A week before leaving the apartment, Paul had greased his little brother with Vaseline. Rachel had quite a time cleaning the stuff out of the little guy's ears and nose, out of the carpet, and off the walls.

Big drops of rain began pounding on the cabin top in the night and continued heavy in the morning, and it was still pouring when Bob and I used the rowboat to get ashore.

Bob, always cheerful, stood on the gravelly beach, skipping stones across the water. I walked some distance away and found a place out of the rain under an overhanging rock ledge. There, I laid on the gravel and fell asleep. Bob was using a stick to bat pebbles forcefully out into the sea when I woke up, but then, coming to my senses, I realized the rain had stopped and the weather had made a decided change. We climbed to a place where it was possible to see that conditions had indeed moderated.

It took only minutes to get back to *The Bowpicker*. The rowboat was lifted to its place and lashed, the engine was started, the anchor was raised, and we were off. By then, it was late afternoon.

Our leaving was somewhat premature; the seas were treacherous outside the mouth of Foggy Bay, but with reduced throttle, we crossed to Danger Passage, and from there, in failing daylight, we reached Ham Island and anchored in a narrow cut at its northwest end.

The evening air had turned pleasantly warm.

The oil stove was started and a proper supper was prepared. Light from the cabin spilled into the cockpit and illuminated the deck and sea near the stern. Little fish, attracted by the glow, flipped and splashed in the water as we ate.

The next morning, we left for Ketchikan, taking turns running the boat and getting dressed in the clean clothes worn in Prince Rupert.

The Bowpicker was tied at the Customs float in Thomas Basin, an area familiar from those when days I had sold newspapers. I climbed the gangway and walked the short distance to the Federal Building and up to the desk, where a matter-of-fact Customs officer asked a few questions and promptly gave us clearance.

From there, we shifted berth to the city floats—a part of Ketchikan even more familiar, since it was there, a dozen years before, that our family had lived on *Gleaner*. Familiar too was the indescribable yet unforgettable rumble of automobile tires rolling on the wooden-planked street above the harbor.

Floats were sturdy and wide, so with no rain, and having space to spread things out, we opened the hatch and pulled burlap bags out to have a look. Knowing all *The Bowpicker* had gone through, it was a relief to find that all was dry, with no hint or smell of mold.

Things were again packed away and the canvas cover secured in place. We set off with bags of dirty duds in search of a laundromat, and in no time, we found one.

Two machines were loaded. A dark blue sweatshirt went into one load and a deep maroon sweatshirt went into the other. Men's cotton underwear and t-shirts only came in *white* in those days. They were equally distributed between loads, with the result being that half of our stuff came out a delicate pink and the other half a dainty blue—a real breakthrough for men's clothing back when TV and decisions were decidedly black and white.

We left Ketchikan the next morning and continued past Guard Island and then Ship Island, in seas calm and most welcome. In the passing hours, the continual drone of the engine in the vastness of Clarence Strait made the day long and most tedious. Coast Guard personnel could be seen moving along the catwalk between the light structure and the buildings that served as quarters at Lincoln Rock. No one waved, and in seven hours, with little change of course, we saw only one other vessel: a far off fishboat.

We continued through Snow Passage then crossed to the top end of Prince of Wales Island to a tiny notch along the shore, where the anchor was lowered.

By then, it was dark.

Just then, the lights of a sizable boat could be seen arriving. Moments later, the rattle of its anchor chain was heard across the water. Bob and I launched the skiff and rowed over. Seeing a light in its pilothouse, I called out and the door swung open. The silhouette of a man invited us in, and we were soon in warm conversation with a person whom it seemed we had always known.

It was pitch black outside when Bob and I climbed down into the rowboat and pushed off. Bright swirls of phosphorescence curled off the ends of the oars as Bob rowed in the direction of *The Bowpicker*'s anchor light.

The alarm went off early. The other vessel had already gone. I started the engine, pulled the anchor, and left. It was still dark while we negotiated the brief passage leading toward Point Colpoys, where a course was set for Wrangell Narrows, fourteen miles away.

Deep purple rays of morning slowly turned to red.

We were perhaps halfway across those fourteen miles when a horrendous line squall blasted across the surface of the sea. *The Bowpicker* was brought around to face it. The engine's rpms were slowed until it passed, and we resumed course and throttle.

The sky slowly turned white, and in time, sleet and tiny flakes began joining the wind.

When at Petersburg, I held the icy nozzle while the tank was topped with gas, We were off again, by now into a swirling world of snowflakes.

Bob and I discussed turning back but reasoned that, if navigation was possible in the blinding fog of British Columbia, it should be just as possible to navigate in snow in Alaska.

Glimpses of Kupreanof Island's shoreline could be seen between flurries.

We'd gone a great distance when the snow finally quit falling, the wind direction changed to a brisk westerly, and the atmosphere became crystal clear. Baronof Island's icy peaks could be clearly seen thirty-some miles to the west. It reminded me of Antarctica.

I was chilled to the core and felt relief going in by the engine, while Bob (bundled in warm clothing) took over steering. Every muscle complained from the hours of standing outside, and now, because of an exaggerated westerly chop, it was necessary to hang on inside.

Daylight was failing as we approached Murder Cove. We went in and tied to a float near a large, time-bleached and deserted building. Moaning sounds, from the wind passing through broken windows, made the place most eerie.

We were soon to bed.

I turned the dome light out, unable to shake the feeling that some crazed savage was outside, waiting to suddenly burst in, but exhaustion prevailed; I fell asleep and slept through the night.

Sixty-Eight Miles

THE ALARM WENT off early as usual. I reached out from my sleeping bag, switched on the overhead light, and lit the oil stove. As soon as it was burning, the kettle was placed on it, as we had done most other mornings. I was up and dressed soon after it began to whistle, but when I stepped outside, huge snowflakes were falling. Thinking of the treacherous reefs on both sides coming into Murder Cove, I stepped back in and gave Bob the report: "Just go back to sleep; I'll call you when it stops snowing."

Once again in the warmth of the cabin, I fell asleep and woke up after 8:00 a.m. Sunlight was streaming in the windows. In moments, I had started the engine, untied, and left. Bob came outside, blinking in the brightness, and asked, "Do you think you waited long enough?"

We continued around the lower end of Admiralty Island and passed fairly close to Point Gardner. Beyond that, a forceful north wind was feeding down the length of Chatham Strait. The seas had not built to any great height, causing us to think that it was merely a short-lived blast of air, so we pushed on.

The wind intensified over the next while, causing spray to be so forceful that it was not possible to look into it and operate the craft.

Bob suggested putting on a diving mask. Why hadn't we thought of that before? Diving equipment was right there in a bag stuffed under the deck in the cockpit; he dug out the mask and handed it to me. I put it on, cinched the rubber strap, and stepped up to the steering platform. It worked perfectly; I had to force myself to not squint into the wind.

When first learning of Bob's offer to make the trip from Seattle, I had purchased double of all of our weather clothing. Shopping was easy; Bob's neck was a bit shorter and his arms a bit longer, but both of us wore the same size of everything. At that particular moment, we were like twins in warm clothing, covered by rain gear, with the exception that he was wearing a knitted cap and I had removed mine to prevent the wind from carrying it away.

Bob reached into the diving bag a second time and pulled out the diving hood. Again, why had the idea not occurred? I pulled it over my head. Now, with the hood and mask, the only area of skin not protected was my bearded chin, which I couldn't keep my hands off of, irritating the area even more.

We reached the Baronof Island side of the strait and continued up that shore out of the main force of the wind, eventually rounding into Warm Springs Bay. When out of the strait, and in the lee of the mountainous land surrounding, we became aware that the weather was actually clear and sunny.

The Bowpicker tied at the only float. After removing layers of clothing, we walked the boardwalk to a small cluster of buildings. Sounds from a marine radio could be heard coming from an open door, where we spoke to a man who had just learned that a tug had been caught by that same powerful wind. Its massive tow of logs had broken up, and the logs had been driven ashore.

We'd heard that hot water seeps from the earth at Warm Springs Bay, so we asked the man about it. He handed each of us a towel and invited us to enjoy the bathhouse.

Hot water ran very slow. Filling would take time, so we set off to hike the short distance to the nearby lake.

I sat and gazed long across its peaceful, frozen surface. Sitka was less than twenty miles away *in a straight line,* but that was no help; the great and treacherous mountains of Baronof Island separated here from there. We needed acceptable weather to continue the remaining eighty-five miles (by boat) to get there.

Again at the bathhouse, tubs were full and the water was quite hot; we eased in slowly.

I woke with a start and called across to Bob, who was asleep in his tub and stirred only after repeated calls. Getting dressed was laborious. The water had robbed us of all our energies.

Our towels were handed back to the man on our way back to *The Bowpicker*, where we continued napping. We were up long enough for supper and then slept through the night.

The next day was clear and beautiful, but when we went out to check, the mighty north wind was still raging, so we returned and tied again to the float.

That was the eighteenth of April, and Bob was scheduled to fly out of Sitka the morning of the twentieth. He would need to report back to army duty. Being late would mar his military record.

The Bowpicker motored out of the bay the next morning. The wind had eased, allowing us to continue northward in Chatham Strait then westward into Peril Strait, finally reaching the zenith of the voyage. From there, our course was to follow the west coast of Baronof Island down to Sitka. Projecting the remaining distance from where we were at that time indicated that we had sixty-eight miles to go.

Bob and I bathed and shaved as we neared Sitka, and once there, the boat was tied to a float long enough for Bob to confirm his flight to Seattle, and also to contact friends who would get him and his stuff to the airplane.

He soon joined me again. I started the engine, and we left, having just one more mile to my parent's island where Rachel and the boys would be.

Drawing near, I could see the color of clothing on the porch, and closer, I could see Rachel waving, and closer yet, I could see Paul and Jim clutching her legs. Somehow in those moments, Seattle seemed long ago and very far away.

BOB WAS DELIVERED back to town the following morning to catch his flight. He went on and fulfilled his obligation to the army. Then he obtained teaching credentials, married Karen, and finally (in 1970), began his dream of teaching in Sitka, and loved it—and his grade 4 students loved him.

That November, he took some fellows hunting. Mistaken for a bear in a snow flurry, he was shot dead by someone in another party and was buried a few days later, a service conducted with all military dignity. I stood and watched as the casket holding the body of my friend ... my friend ... my friend Bob, age thirty-three, as it was slowly lowered into the ground. His father and two other men came and held me. They seemed to understand.

Small Island Life

Now that our move from Seattle had been made, Rachel and I, with our little ones, were ready to set up for life in the empty dwelling on Morne Island.

Just as Frank and Nancy had acquired that island by means of the Homesite Act, my parents and their friends Bob and Maude Simpson had acquired small, unnamed islands very close by. The three islands were linked by CB radio Channel 6.

Frank was part owner of Tri-Ways Marina, a floating facility in the channel separating Mount Edgecombe from Sitka. His move to Jamestown Bay put him and his family on Sitka's road system, which was handy to his responsibilities at the marina.

Part of the marina's floating facilities included a sizable barge, sunken down to the height of the rest of its floats, all of which were held in place by well-positioned pilings. Customers arriving by boat could tie to a float or to the barge. Those coming by land used the gangplank.

A sizable building had been placed on the barge as a shop for repairing boats, which was the shop I'd be attending, but first, before setting up shop, there were things I needed to do.

Earlier, when Frank and Nancy lived on Morne Island, they simply beached their open boat in front of their cabin. *The Bowpicker* would need a proper float and gangplank, and the best place for it was on the south side of the island next to a vertical face having deep water right up to it.

I immediately set about installing a solid wooden beam across the vee indentation in that rock face—not an easy job, having no good place to stand while using a sizable hammer in the right hand and a rock drill in the left to pound holes in anticipation of using one-inch-diameter steel pins to secure the beam to the rock.

When that was in place, I ran two more heavy beams back into the vee and likewise pinned them to the rock. Additional structure was added to support decking at a height carefully calculated for the highest tides and greatest storm conditions.

After completing the work in the vee, I constructed three twenty-foot-long sections of float and a gangplank. The outer end of the three floats were to be secured by chain to a rock that was exposed at low tide. This meant drilling another hole, always at night when tides were lowest, always feeling vulnerable working alone by flashlight in the dark. The final touch to the installation was to build a stairway from the deck to the trail that led through the woods to the cabin.

Rachel and I were given a galley range for the cabin with the apology that nobody could make it burn right. Constant oil heat works like wood heat to dispel the dampness and chill that prevails in coastal Alaska in cooler months. I sought the insight of the local marine hardware supplier, Pete Hogan, who gave good instruction and supplied the things to fix it. I followed his direction exactly, and when finished, lit the range, not turning it off again until the following spring. The fire clay was still clean.

Living on Morne Island meant living close with nature where we could

easily catch fish, and with diving equipment, I could easily gather things that lived under the sea: crabs, urchins, sea cucumbers, and rock scallops. Earlier village life gave the advantage of knowing what could be eaten from the tidal zone or from the beach or the area above it: sun-dried seaweed, wild asparagus, and a special kind of grass called goose tongue that was used to make tasty salads.

That summer, Frank set up a diesel-powered generator on the pier. Wires were strung through the forest to our cabin, and a cable was laid on the sea floor to link the islands belonging to my parents and the Simpsons.

Having electrical power was a wonderful addition, especially during those months when days were short and nights were long. Like most any home-generator system, power was on for a limited time each evening.

Having a flashlight in the back pocket was normal to island life, but we also commonly used kerosene lanterns. With kerosene, one has both light and heat. A lantern would sometimes be placed beside *The Bowpicker*'s engine at the end of day, and the next morning, the boat's cabin would be warm and the engine would start easily.

One morning, on my way to town, I came upon a mess of lumber that had apparently washed off the deck of a ship. I returned and got Rachel, and together, we gathered enough to add a sizable porch outside the door of the cabin.

I built a proper pilothouse on *The Bowpicker* that fall, which allowed the boat to be operated from *inside*. Having sliding doors on both sides made it possible to lean out and tie up on either side.

The Bowpicker was handy in every way. It served as daily transportation to the shop in town and provided an "office" in which to keep paperwork and special products. Having a covered forward hold made it possible to keep larger items dry, and the hatch cover itself was a nice flat area.

Two fellows arrived at the marina with a huge outboard motor needing to go in for repair. It was past business hours, and the place was closed, so I agreed to deliver it the next morning. The three of us wrestled it onto *The Bowpicker*'s flat hatch cover, and I carefully blocked it to prevent its tipping or sliding.

The next morning, I untied and left for work in town. The chop was short and steep in the channel. *The Bowpicker*'s bow rose and fell as expected, but then the big motor suddenly popped straight up out of its blocking and tumbled into the sea.

I felt sick and was still in shock when I told the marina people what had happened. One of the marina owners, Ed Martin, assured me that the mishap would surely be covered by insurance.

Thank God, it was.

Alaska Tidal Wave

I PUT IN my days at the boat shop, and Rachel put in her days on the island with the boys. She did not like slugs, and there were a lot of them around our Morne Island cabin. Each day she'd go out with an ax and saw and remove brush. In time, she had that whole area cleared, which gave a better view and let in more light. Light discouraged the slugs, so they moved back into the more densely shaded forest.

Using tools day after day caused her to become immensely strong. One day, she hugged me enthusiastically, and when she did, with her arms just below my rib cage, I nearly collapsed.

Work at the boat shop was steady. Most boats that Sitkans used were built in the States, and most were made of fiberglass. Few manufactures understood conditions in Alaska and how seriously boats were used. Much of my work was to fix things that broke or install things like proper cleats.

Many jobs were more involved, such as repairing or replacing a double bottom, reinforcing a transom, or repairing a bash, gash, or split. There were also orders for control pedestals and cabin enclosures.

There were challenges; low temperatures and high humidity were usually outside the range of product formulations, which meant that heat lamps were needed to boost temperatures.

I sometimes had John's help.

John was a tall, good-looking man originally from Pigeon Cove, Massachusetts. His accent was typical of that region. He occasionally talked about a "latin." How he used the word didn't make sense, so I asked him to spell it, and he did: "L-a-n-t-e-r-n."

John also taught me about "souners." As it turned out, he was talking about "saunas." Just why New Englanders learned to leave r's out of some words and add them to others will always be a mystery.

John was our good neighbor back in Renton in the Boeing days, and he already owned the stout thirty-foot-long Tahiti ketch *Kaloa* before I bought *The Bowpicker*. It was only after Bob and I left Seattle that John felt the challenge to venture beyond local waters. He bought charts to go to Hawaii or Alaska and severed ties with Seattle before deciding which place he would go.

It came as a pleasant surprise and grand reunion of friends when *Kaloa* arrived and dropped anchor next to Morne Island. His vessel remained at anchor over the following weeks. John would often row his eight-foot-long dingy to Sitka, visit and help in my shop, then row the full mile of oar strokes back to *Kaloa*. One day, a massive sea lion came up behind his dingy with its neck outstretched, trying to look inside. John pulled *Koloa*'s anchor shortly after that and tied at the marina.

He would often come into the boat shop wearing white coveralls with the sole purpose of helping, and he truly was a handy help, with manners well suited for meeting and talking with people.

I was down inside a boat in the shop, and working in an awkward position, when I heard two voices. One asked, "Do you remember me?"

John's voice answered, "No, I don't."

After some hesitation, the other voice replied, "I don't remember you either."

Boy, I thought, *these guys aren't making much sense.* So I emerged to see what was going on. The explanation was simple: The man had remembered my family in Ketchikan years earlier, and when he learned I was in the shop, he had walked in expecting me.

EVERYTHING CHANGED ON Friday, March 27, 1964. The day started as usual at the boat shop, but the afternoon hours seemed weighty under a heavy pewter sky. Nature became strangely hushed, with no wind, no rain, no birds, and no explanation.

I was looking forward to the Good Friday service at the church and had nice clothes to change into.

My father and mother, and neighbors Bob and Maude, would be coming from their islands in Dad's boat, and Bob had his car, so they'd pick me up from the street above the shop. Plans were to leave *The Bowpicker* tied where it was over the weekend, and I'd hitch a ride into town with Dad on Monday.

Rachel wanted to remain at the cabin so the boys could be put to bed at their regular time.

It was dark and pouring rain when we came out of church and continued as we ran from the car at Thompson Harbor. The rain was swallowing most of the light from a single bulb on a pole at the end of the pier. I pulled the flashlight from my rear pocket to assist the steps of others as they descended the unusually steep gangway, but I also momentarily shone its beam down on the mucky low-tide beach below. *Surely,* I thought, *this is not right. Low tide was hours ago.*

Everyone was soon inside Dad's cruiser and under cover. I let the boat's lines go when I heard the engine start.

He maneuvered the craft out of the breakwater and into the darkness. Light from town provided shafts of low illumination in the channel, yet I sensed that something strange was happening; I was sure low tide had been in the afternoon. The sea was swirling and the dark silhouette of harbor rocks, usually submerged, could be seen standing several feet above the surface.

We hadn't felt the 9.2 magnitude earthquake that had occurred in the area between Valdez and Anchorage and didn't know that a tsunami had been created, the effects of which were just then reaching our shore.

It simultaneously dawned on Dad and I that we were experiencing the recession of sea that occurs before a tidal wave. He maneuvered out of the narrow channel into less turbulent waters and to the float shared by Bob and Maude and my parents.

From there, still raining hard, I used Mom's thirteen-foot-long Boston Whaler (small open boat) to motor the short distance across to Morne Island. Once there, I started the generator, switched on all circuits, and hurried through the forest trail to tell Rachel what was going on. Having no idea the size of the wave to come, I asked her to collect some items just in case we needed to move to higher ground.

Paul and Jim were peacefully asleep.

I hurried through the trail to the float and sat, dressed as I was for the church service, in the open boat in the dark and pouring rain. The sound of the running generator and lights were a comfort.

I watched as the sea began to rise, inch by inch, until it covered the marks I'd painted on the rocks when building the deck. It then stopped and began receding.

Cold rainwater that had pooled in my underwear poured down my pant legs when I stood to go and give Rachel the report.

That was the first wave.

After changing into dry and more appropriate clothing, I returned and watched the second wave, higher than the first, come to the exact height of the deck where the generator was running. I was about to go and stop the engine when the sea began ever-so slowly to recede.

There was no keeping track of the hour as the third wave came and went. Being lower than the first two, I returned to the cabin and fell asleep, fully dressed, with the generator running through the night.

Sitka was largely spared, but there was significant damage in and about the harbor. John's *Kaloa* had been pushed against a cluster of fiberglass boats, but he managed to drag his dingy to an open space of water and get to the beach. He and a willing high-school kid got to *The Bowpicker* and ran it to safety.

The marina sustained a lot of damage. The boat shop was destroyed by water, perhaps five feet deep, which had flooded across the deck of the barge. The bandsaw was on its side. Nails, screws, extension cords, portable lights, and power tools were spread about, and three boats under repair were pushed into a heap in one corner.

Small craft surrounding the marina were damaged, many having been swamped and some overturned. John's *Kaloa* was not damaged. *The Bowpicker* took some damages, but none that were difficult to repair.

Over the next days, I cut the ends out of several steel oil drums and filled them with fresh water. Everything electric was submerged and brought home a few pieces at a time and dried on the oven door. Most everything was made to work again, but even so, I felt that it was time to pack up and carry on with … well … the next chapter.

The Old Atlas Diesel

DICK NELSON HAD been well known to our family since the early 1950s. He was running the tug *Inverness,* which would occasionally tie at the wharf opposite the boat shop, where he and I were able to visit across the water.

The owners of that tug and others of the fleet, were brothers George and Louie Baggen of Samson Tug and Barge. George was a fine-featured, disciplined man. He ran the tug *Martin D* and coordinated everything by medium-frequency marine radio from the vessel's two-story pilothouse. His brother Louie was a heavy, round-faced, cigar-smoking, predominantly one-eyed man with a carefree swagger. I later learned that he was blind in the lesser eye. He ran the picture-perfect tug *Samson.* The brothers were as different as night and day, yet each in their own way were greatly to be admired.

After the tsunami, I was visiting Dick on his tug when Louie also happened to arrive. Somehow, in the mix of Dick knowing me and my family and Louie knowing my father, I was automatically hired on as mate.

Some days before leaving port, I went aboard *Inverness* to better acquaint myself with the vessel and its systems. No one was there. After looking over the deck equipment, I went into the pilothouse and noted that everything was conventional except for the big Bendix radar. That would take some learning.

A well-illustrated manual for the tug's massive six-cylinder Atlas Imperial diesel engine was found in a locker near the chart table. I opened it and studied through several pages, then went down into the engine room to reinforce my learning by looking at the real thing; most parts on those old engines were open and visible.

I was partway through the manual when Louie Baggen and Dick Nelson stepped aboard, and by coincidence, were talking about a portion of the book

I had just studied. Having an understanding look on my face must have triggered something in Louie. Partway through a sentence, he stopped, studied me carefully with his good eye, and with a tone of finality in his deep, gravelly voice said, "You'll be the engineer on this tug too."

So, it was Dick, myself, and a third fellow to cook and help on deck, not expected to stand a watch or know about running the vessel.

Over the following months, I became intimately familiar with that big Atlas and everything else on the tug, as well as the surrounding geography. Logs were towed at walking pace day and night over great expanses of southeastern Alaska.

Old-school protocol strictly prohibited sitting while in the pilothouse and steering. The *Inverness* pilothouse didn't have a place to sit, which was a good thing. Drowsiness caused by the sound and feel of that big, slow-turning engine in the wee hours would surely have put a sitting person to sleep. I'd sometimes plant my chin on my doubled fist on the spoke of the wheel. When sleep occurred, my fist would relax and my chin would drop—fortunately never enough to bash it on the wooden spoke. Those little nod-offs kept me going through many long sleep-deprived nights.

One day, sitting at the galley table, my eyes focused on a blue pharmaceutical-looking bottle of Alka-Seltzer on the shelf. Its label instructed one to place a tablet in a glass and add water. Drinking the water while it effervesced was said to bring relief to a number of maladies, including headache.

A plaguing headache some nights later triggered the thought of that blue bottle. It was a good time to test its fizzy wonders. *Inverness* was running free (not towing) in darkness in Peril Strait. The radar was keeping a good view, and it was a calm night. I went to the galley, opened the bottle, dropped a tablet into a porcelain mug, and added water. As it foamed, I brought the cup to my lips, began drinking, and fainted.

I don't know why.

First cognition was the sound of the big Atlas. I was the only one awake and hurried back to the pilothouse where I studied the radar image. All was well and somehow the headache was less important.

Things sometimes *do* go wrong. One day, we were coupling log booms (rafts) in preparation for towing them through Sergius Narrows. An unusual feel about the tug triggered a search that led to the realization that a significant amount of seawater had accumulated in the engine room. We secured to the logs, set about investigating, and soon found out that something had  penetrated the heavy hull. We couldn't stop the water coming in.

I always carried my diving wetsuit and mask on the tug, so I suited up and went into the sea to have a look from the outside. The toggle of a boom chain had pushed through a spot some inches below the waterline where hardwood sheathing had (at some point in the life of the tug) been compromised.

I remained in the water, and Dick handed down whatever was needed to plug the leak, starting with rags and gobs of water pump grease. He then fashioned a wooden plug that I managed to pound into the hole with a sledgehammer (understand that it is not possible to swing a hammer underwater).

The plug was sawed off flush and covered with a thickness of sheet lead, secured with closely spaced copper tacks.

Little thought was given to that patch over the following months, until the tug was hauled out of the water in Juneau. There, an old Scottish shipwright was given the job of repairing the breach properly.

The name *Inverness* was like music to the man. I heard him breathing the word as he was beginning the job.

I told him what had happened and how Dick and I had made the repair. He listened closely, but after progressing into the work, he eyed me askance and muttered in a scolding Scottish brogue, "Could not have been done in the water."

Inverness was secured that December, and Dick was assigned to run *Lillian S*. That automatically made me both mate and engineer. Again, we had a third fellow. The assignment was to tow a fuel barge around southeastern Alaska, serving the needs of mostly dormant logging camps.

Barge towing is very different than log towing. With logs, you untie and pull and little happens, but with patience and by working with tidal currents, the logs eventually get where they are supposed to go. With a barge, you simply untie and go where you want.

One day in Frederick Sound, a great tempest arose, whipping the sea into vapor. *Lillian S* began taking on water to the degree that pumps were barely keeping up. I crawled through bilges with a flashlight trying without success to determine where the water was coming in. When out of the strong wind, the leaking stopped. This caused me to suspect that the problem was above the water line, and upon investigation, we found that air-vent pipes projecting through the mid and forward portion of the deck had rusted out on their unpainted backsides. I wrapped sheet metal around each one and secured the sheeting with haywire—enough to get the tug safely through the winter.

Lillian S was a comfortable vessel with a second-story pilothouse set back of a cargo hold. The galley was on the main deck with Dutch doors on both sides.

Two or three of the company tugs would sometimes raft together, and when they did, *Lillian S* was the natural gathering place. One fellow, Tommy—a good-spirited fellow originally from Vancouver Island—sometimes played his accordion. It was a rare treat to hear music of any kind in a world of remote log towing.

The whole Samson fleet was equipped with top-of-the-line Bendix radars, and *Lillian S* had the best, with clarity down to a quarter mile. At that range, the center dot appeared as a little circle.

Using that circle was the case one snowy night, towing in Olga Strait, when nothing could be seen through pilothouse windows. The water depth was good up to the beach, so I brought the little round radar circle (and therefore the tug) and its tow close to the shore to minimize the effect of the opposing current.

Curious at one point, I wondered if the bright shaft of light from my flashlight could penetrate through the swirling flakes enough to see the near gravel beach. I leaned out the open side window and switched it on. It came as a surprise to see how very close we were.

Adjustment was made to give a wider margin.

It was just then, of all times, that the radar quit! I noted the compass heading and brought the ship's track a few degrees to the right, assuming it would keep the tug and logs off the beach. After slowing the engine, I went and roused Dick. There was nothing either of us could do, but he was the captain and needed to know what was happening.

After several tense minutes, like magic, the radar came on again! There was an explanation: A tour through the engine room revealed that the manual rheostat controlling the battery-charge rate was set too low, and the radar, apparently protecting itself from low voltage, had shut itself down. When battery voltage recovered, it switched on again.

Winter-fuel barge towing with *Lillian S* came to an end in early spring, and Dick and I went back to log towing with *Inverness*.

The largest tug of the company's fleet, *Martin D*, was towing a huge coupling of log rafts (booms) in Salisbury Sound with *Inverness* lashed to the logs and lending its Atlas muscle to the towing. Hours continued into a crisp moonlit night, where everything outside was high-definition black and silver.

Lanterns secured on jack stands were burning at intervals across the front, middle, and rear of the massive tow. Such lighting was (and is) a navigational requirement. It seemed a good time to fill lantern reservoirs with kerosene. I stepped from the guard of the *Inverness* and onto the logs, flashlight in one hand and kerosene container and funnel in the other, and was off to fill each lantern and adjust each flame.

When finished, I began the trek back to the tug. Being such a lovely, bright, big round silver-moonlit night, I chose to walk the outer-side sticks. Suddenly, like a surrealistic scene in a horror movie, the gigantic body of an orca rose up next to me. It was perhaps attracted to the flashlight.

Heart pounding with fright, I hurried to get away, knowing one misstep would have me down in the inky black sea with the creature. Mine was a blessed relief when I reached the deck of *Inverness* still alive to hear the sound of its old Atlas Imperial diesel engine and feel the pulse of its pistons beneath my feet.

The Happy Board

WITH LOG TOWING, there was a seasonal drive to keep things moving, and that meant towing from faraway places and being away from home for long periods of time.

Since logs ended up at the pulp mill at Silver Bay, *Inverness* occasionally towed past Morne Island where Rachel and our little guys were. Such was the case one morning in late June 1965.

I studied the shore through the pilothouse windows, and there appeared to be something of color on the shore. I stepped out with binoculars and had a better look. It was Rachel and the boys, and they were holding up two signs. I steadied myself to make out the words. One said, "HAPPY." I strained to see the lettering on the other, and then it suddenly became clear: "ANNIVERSARY."

I felt a stab of sorrow for myself, but even more for Rachel, who had only the children to talk to. She had CB radio channel 6, and people on that channel could communicate, but radio was no substitute for having at least *some* first-hand time with other adults.

My dream before the tsunami had been to build a house on Morne Island with a gazebo-like living room that faced Kruzof Island's sleeping volcano. Imagination pictured its foundation anchored into solid rock above the float, where we could look down and see *The Bowpicker* in its place. That dream was most certainly not coming together, and there was no prospect that it ever would.

In time, Rachel learned to operate *The Bowpicker* and did a good job of it, which gave her freedom to go to and from town. On one occasion, however, arriving at the float on the island, she made a landing in fierce wind, jumped off with a midship line, then watched in horror as a great gust caught *The Bowpicker* and began carrying it away, its engine idling out of gear, and with the children inside. Thinking fast, she managed to scramble on at the bow and again take control.

After the "HAPPY ANNIVERSARY" incident, we rented a place in town. The boys adjusted well, and Rachel began filling in as receptionist and secretary in Dr. Edward Spencer's office. She had become so used to using radio that she had to catch herself on the phone before saying the word "over" at the end of every sentence.

The Bowpicker was sold, complete with everything, to a family that found great pleasure cruising in southeastern Alaska over following summers, and in the long of things, they enjoyed it for the rest of its fifty-some years of life.

I continued working on *Inverness* through the long busy summer.

It was my habit to always carry a Bible with my stuff on the tug; a lot of sailors do that. If nothing else, it serves as a good-luck charm.

Several company tugs were together one day when I had my Bible open on the galley table trying to understand something in the Book of Matthew.

One of the guys came in and asked, "What's *that*?"

I turned the cover and pointed at the words, "Holy Bible."

"What are you doing with *that*?" he persisted.

"I'm *trying* to read it," I said. "I can't figure out what the words mean."

He asked to see, and then began reading partly aloud while muttering words such as, "Oh yes," and "uh-huh," suggesting that he understood. I felt cheated, thinking that it was *me* trying to read the Bible, and *this* guy who comes in half scoffing seems to understand it.

The longer story is that Bible studies broke out among the guys on the different tugs. One fellow, the least you'd guess to read the Bible, had enough theological knowledge to intelligently answer most any questions.

I WAS HOSPITALIZED at the Mount Edgecombe Government Hospital late that September, crippled and bent because of scrambling on logs carrying heavy boom chains. First, X-rays were taken, then infrared treatments were used to relax seized muscles and ease the pain. I was ordered to complete bed rest and strictly told not to continue the same job activity.

Heavy work was one thing, and I understood I wouldn't be able to keep doing the same job, but my appreciation for the beauty of the coast was something I dearly wanted to share with Rachel and our boys as family fun.

While still largely bedridden, I contacted a boat broker in Vancouver BC, first by phone and then by letter, describing what I was looking for in a boat. Back pain was a gnawing affliction but tolerable enough that I thought we could travel there. Money earned in Alaska made travel and buying in Canada advantageous.

By then, 1965, Alaska had ferry service and our first leg of travel was to Prince Rupert.

Paul was five and Jim was three.

My injured back continued to nag, making me irritable. Upon arrival, I got into a tiff with the Customs officer when he demanded plans for our time in Prince Rupert. I told him I had none and that we simply wanted to enjoy the city a few days before flying to Vancouver. He wasn't happy with my answer, and I wasn't happy with him, so I said, quite forcefully, "We'll be on the first plane out of here in the morning."

Flight plans were easily made, and we got a room for the night. I contacted the boat broker in Vancouver and let him know we were coming.

We were sitting in the airport waiting room the next morning when a courteous, well-dressed man walked up and politely asked, "Mr. Getman?"

"Yes, sir," I answered.

"Follow me," he said, and attentively led us to our places in the plane. Others were allowed to board only after we were comfortably seated.

I've often wondered if that extra measure of courtesy had to do with Customs or something extended by the airline for people with small children.

Either way, it was bye-bye, Prince Rupert.

Upon arriving in Vancouver, we were welcomed by Nigel Rothwell, a well-mannered, tweed-suited boat broker who drove us to the English Hotel. Being unaccustomed with moving at car speed in traffic, I became carsick (not enough to throw up), and when arriving at the hotel with agonizing back pain, I gladly accepted his help with the luggage.

Nigel and I were ready to talk business the next day. My earlier communications so much described a particular boat that Nigel had told its owners, Ralph and Bea Vittery. They made it clear their boat was not for sale. Now that we had come all the way from Alaska, Nigel said that he would contact them again. He did, and Ralph gave Nigel permission to show us their ketch, *Ivanhoe*, and told him where the key was hidden—but we were only to *see* it. Ralph emphasized that it was *not* for sale.

Ivanhoe was simply beautiful. Thirty-eight feet on the deck, it *did* fit the description of what I was looking for, but that didn't make it for sale. Nigel phoned owner Ralph again. Since we had come all the way from Alaska, Ralph was now curious about us and requested that we join him and Bea for supper at their home in North Vancouver.

Bea was an elegant woman and gracious hostess. Ralph was a solid-faced, nautically knowledgeable fellow. He made his living as an independent shipwright.

It was easy understanding why they didn't want to sell their boat; they had enjoyed summers cruising with their now-adult children, Alan and Joan. It was clear that *Ivanhoe* was deeply woven into the family's heart.

Paul and Jim were as captivated as Rachel and I were by the many family cruising stories and photos in a big picture album.

Ralph and Bea excused themselves and remained absent from the room for an awkward length of time. Their faces were strangely solemn when they returned. It made no sense to me when Ralph asked if they could keep the ship's clock. I suddenly realized that they had decided to sell their precious *Ivanhoe*.

Ivanhoe was a documented Canadian vessel. To sell it was one thing but to transfer documentation from Canada to U.S. documentation was quite another. We remained in Vancouver over the following weeks while collaborating agents worked out details to make it happen.

That wait was a blessing, allowing us precious family time enjoying exquisite gardens, parks, beaches, and the zoo. That time also gave my sore back time to much recover.

Zoo visits were frequent—so frequent that I made friends with one of the seals in the large circular pool. Stonewalls were too high to reach down and touch the little guy, but whenever I arrived, he readily responded to my voice and swam up close. Rachel made friends with a shy little monkey named Janey at the primate cages. Janey would immediately recognize Rachel and reach out her little hand and shyly hold Rachel's.

Vancouver also had its cinemas, which were playing *Mary Poppins*, starring Julie Andrews and Dick Van Dyke, and also *My Fair Lady*, which held the distinction of being the longest-running theatre production in history. We also saw *Chitty Chitty Bang Bang*, which was an entertaining story about a magical car.

Vancouver was a great place with beautiful department stores and unlimited selection. Rachel and I bought clothes, stocked *Ivanhoe*'s lockers, and bought Lego blocks for the boys, making sure there were plenty. While waiting those weeks, we also had time to sail and cruise about freely.

One lovely morning, we came around the north end of Bowen Island under full sail and set a course to pass close off Point Atkinson. The wind was out of the northeast, blowing around twenty. Rachel had made pancakes, and when finished, she came up to steer while I went in to eat. The boys had already eaten and were in their forward quarters, happily playing on the carpeted floor.

I could see Rachel's face outside the open door from where I was sitting and enjoying the pancakes. I noted the hint of concern in her expression. She asked me to come up, but I continued eating, since by the feel of things there was no reason for apprehension.

She called down again, so this time I emerged and discovered that *Ivanhoe* was surrounded by monstrous angry tide rips. This was my introduction to the great steadying power of wind in sail. We quickly dropped the main and continued under jib and mizzen.

November in Howe Sound Canada was much like summer in southeastern Alaska, so being fresh off tugs, a t-shirt top seemed appropriate. Sailing in winds of twenty or twenty-five knots, and even greater at times, seemed normal and natural. Tacking to windward had its limits however. Mentioning it later to Ralph, he said, "Roy, no one is out there sailing for fun in weather like that."

How would I know? It was a common thing when living on Morne Island to commute in winds thirty-five or more.

Paperwork pertaining to *Ivanhoe* was completed in November. We carried on under sail and power to Seattle, and secured at 2100 West Commodore Way. This was beautiful and tranquil Salmon Bay Marina, inside the locks in fresh water, so of course, there was no tide. *Ivanhoe* was given a prime place, tight against the bulkhead next to heaven's shore. Two relaxed willow trees stood in a posture of perpetual gratitude a dozen yards away.

ᵍHello Honolulu

THE SAILBOAT DREAM had come true. I now needed to accept the reality that I needed to find a job.

I walked to the Foss office and spoke with the man behind the counter. "Do you have need for an A.B? (a fully licensed seaman). My endorsement was for *Tugs and Towboats Any Waters Unlimited.* He hired me on the spot, even though I said I had a bad back.

It was December 15, 1965 when I stepped on board the one-hundred-twenty-seven-foot-long Miki-class tug *Barbara Foss,* with my sea bag and joined the eleven others readying for towing to Honolulu. We left shortly and headed to Everett to take charge of a three-hundred-twenty-five-foot-long barge whose three cargo holds had been filled with lumber and wood products.

The tug's stern was brought up under the big blunt bow of the barge, giving the impression that it was very solid and seaworthy. The deck crew set about attaching towing gear. Everything about coupling for ocean towing is done with most exacting precision.

The tug was to leave Puget Sound, finish loading at a terminal in the Columbia River, and then deliver everything to Honolulu.

Barbara Foss left Everett, travelled seaward out the Strait of Juan de Fuca, rounded Cape Flattery, and carried on down the coast and into the Columbia River. Normally, a pilot would be required for the river, but in this case, the tug's master, Captain Tauno Salo, was a licensed pilot for the Columbia.

River current is a consideration for landing a bulky barge, but all good arrangement had been made. Two small tugs were on hand to assist the landing.

Loading operations came to a standstill over Christmas. The tug's crew milled about in the low lighting of the galley. The cook made eggnog (bless him), a genuine gesture of Christmas cheer. I had neither the eggnog nor the cheer.

Lumber and timbers were placed as a deck load on the barge over the following days. It formed a towering deck load needing to be lashed with lengths of chain for winter towing.

The wind was filled with icy rain and wet snow, making it impossible to keep warm. One would *think* the combination of being warmly dressed and the strenuous work of lashing would dispel the cold, but no, this was the Columbia River Gorge, which channels a type of chill that penetrates all rules of reason.

Eventually, all the chains, shackles, and turnbuckles were in place. Lashings were then brought up tight, one by one, with many hands working together, as though we were tuning the strings of a giant cello.

Tug and barge left the Columbia on December 31, 1965, the night that turned to January 1, 1966. This was before satellite monitoring and computer modeling, so predicting weather mostly meant sniffing the air and watching the barometer.

We were fully committed to the Pacific when the ship's radio urgently warned of an approaching storm of hurricane force. The great blast arrived in hours and continued for days. It was a tempest that ripped the ocean to shreds—a ravage of nature beyond worded description.

The tug was cruelly tossed, rising and falling thirty or more feet, and rolling fifty and fifty-five degrees.

I became violently seasick and began to hallucinate. I'd be in a brief state of reality, then be looking across a lush green field with white fences and horses grazing beside a misty lake.

Steering meant only keeping the bow of the tug to the wind, while its deep, slow-turning propeller kept it separated from its tow.

Captain Salo, most kindly and understandingly, excused me from my station to vomit when I needed to. This meant leaving the wheel, and getting safely down the stairs and to the garbage can lashed in the galley.

At one point, I was down on my knees with my elbows locked inside the can, its lid sliding around behind me. I found it most comforting watching the greenish goo just brought up from my stomach swirling gently around with coffee grounds in the bottom of the can.

Only the faintest illumination served as daylight the next morning, while the wind continued to drive waves to massive heights. It was possible, with binoculars, to see that chain lashings had let go and most of the deck load had spilled into the sea. Occasional glimpses of yellow-brown lumber could be seen surrounding the barge.

That burly barge had looked *so* solid and confident in Everett, but on this dispirited day, great lengths of its flat bottom could be seen in its rolling. Steel uprights, meant to help hold the deck  load, were twisted and bent. Some were torn away, leaving ruptures in the deck plating.

Captain Salo remained continually in the pilothouse, wedged in a spot near the chart table with a gooseneck lamp pulled down so that he could read a cowboy book. I asked how he could be so cool. His answer was brief: "There's nothing else I can do." He then added, "No Miki class tug has ever turned over."

Wind and wave began to ease over the next days, and I began to crave popcorn. Maybe it was the salt. Salty crackers were tried but I could only blow dust—no saliva. Sucking soft tomatoes seemed to help.

The tug, with its crippled tow, was eventually brought into the protection of the outer breakwater at Crescent City, California. A considerable length of towline was allowed to rest on the sea floor in the shape of a big arc, which effectively anchored both tug and barge.

The following day, workboats from the port assisted the *Barbara Foss* and its barge to a wharf. We worked side by side with salvage crews bailing flooded compartments and putting things in enough order to carry on to Honolulu.

Weather slowly became spring-like over the next fifteen days, as we moved into warmer latitudes.

Once secured in Honolulu, sea watches were broken while stevedores worked to unload the barge. That gave us freedom to be tourists.

I went into a department store with the thought of finding a Hawaiian-style dress for Rachel and Hawaiian shirts for Paul and Jim. Not knowing what sizes she or the boys wore, and feeling awkward in the dress section, I approached a petit sales clerk. "Pardon me, please, I'm a sailor on a tug. You may be able to help me pick out a Hawaiian-style dress for my wife in Seattle." Continuing, I said, "You appear to be her same height and build." I also told the lady what I had in mind for the boys. She asked their ages and then walked away. After a time, she returned with a lovely blue-flowered muumuu (dress) and two matching blue-flowered shirts.

The dress later proved to look stunning on Rachel, and the shirts were especially attractive on the boys.

Those Miki-class tugs were round-bottomed and seaworthy, but also rolly. One day, on the seventeen-day return to the mainland from Hawaii, the mate told me he had a problem, and asked if I would come into his quarters and listen. An annoying sound was coming from the ceiling. He knew that I knew carpentry, because I had installed shelves in the ship's pantry and made deck chairs from salvaged materials on the way to Honolulu.

I could hear what sounded like a loose wood screw. Roll, roll, roll, roll. The ongoing sound day and night was driving him daffy. For a time, the sound would stop (it was assumed that the screw would turn sideways), and then roll, roll, roll again.

I told him there was no way to take the ceiling apart, but *something* had to be done. He went to the engine room, got a hand drill, returned to his room, and drilled a little hole in the ceiling. Next, he went to the galley and got the honey thing—you know, the plastic squeeze bottle with a tapered tip. He took it up to his room, and when he heard the screw rolling, he stuck the honey tip into the hole and gave it a big squeeeeeeeeze. Sudden silence. That was the end of the irritating roll, roll, roll.

Hallelujah and amen!

WE HAD BARGED a military cargo back to San Francisco. When that was delivered, we then carried on to Seattle. All counted, Seattle to Seattle was sixty-five days, with a towing speed that was just a bit faster than walking.

That towing was long ago. Now there's a much more modern *Barbara Foss,* heavier than its predecessor, with more horsepower. A few summers ago, I was running *Coastal Messenger* in Alaska when an announcement was sounded on VHF radio. It was the new *Barbara Foss* with its huge barge southbound in Tongass Narrows. We were northbound. Quickly calculating, it was evident that the two vessels would meet at the narrowest place. I asked Joan (nickname Petunia)—a proficient radio operator—to contact the tug and say that *Coastal Messenger* would keep off to the side and give *Barbara Foss* and the tow the whole channel.

She did this and got a ho-hum acknowledgement, but she then mentioned that her skipper (me) was presently in the pilothouse and had served on the old *Barbara Foss.* The voice on the other end became animated, saying, "Wow, he must be a lot older than me."

The vessels drew near in passing, and as they did, figures from the tug's pilothouse came out and stood on the wing. Simultaneously, several from the deckhouse below came out and lined the rail, all standing in a posture of respect.

What was that about? It's hard to explain, but in short, it's not just the journey or the job. There is a great unspoken coterie that exists in the hearts of those who are linked by the many coasts and waters of this world.

ᚠruitless Alaska

AFTER THAT WINTER trip on *Barbara Foss*, I went to the Foss office and asked for something not so long away from family. I was assigned to the one-hundred-seventeen-foot-long tug *Wedell Foss*, which ran three trips a month towing a rail barge between Bellingham, Washington, and Ward Cove, Alaska. I'd be home between trips.

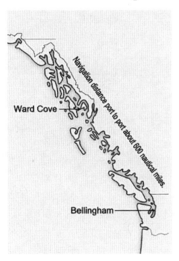

At age twenty-six, I was by far the youngest on the tug. Her captain, Ed Paine, was a solid square-jawed fellow. I was to be the sailor on his eight-to-twelve watches, morning and night. "This job separates the men from the boys," he repeated several times while showing me around.

I was put to work with the others lashing boxcars in the process of readying for sea; he scrutinized my every move and again repeated the words, "This job separates the men from the boys." There was a routine, and the men followed it wordlessly.

The tug and tow was eventually out and away from Bellingham, and those off watch retired from the deck. One of the guys quietly prompted me regarding deck procedures and warned that the captain was strict to every detail.

In those days, tugs used heavy tires as bumpers along the greater length of their hulls. In the case of the *Wedell Foss*, some were bolted permanently in place near the bow, but those farther back were hung on chains to drop over guards and then lifted and lashed when readying for sea.

The *Wedell Foss* was what is called a formal vessel. Oh, I knew the formalities—I *had* to know all that stuff for my A.B. certification and that included bridge etiquette.

I carefully checked *everything* before climbing the stairs to the bridge, opened the door (the captain was steering), and gained permission to enter. Once granted, I asked, "Would you have me steer, sir?"

With unyielding eyes on me, he said, "Oh, you think you are ready to steer?" His voice was filled with disdain.

"Yes, sir," I answered.

He then began quizzing me regarding the deck, with most sentences starting with, "Tell me..." or "Did you..."

"Yes, sir," I repeated after every question.

After long hesitation, and with defiant chin and squinting eyes, the captain asked, "Tell me, did you check the lifeboat cover?"

I confirmed that I had.

"Tell me then," he queried, "what kind of knots did you find?"

"Quick-release knots, sir," I answered.

"Very well," he said, looking scarcely convinced. "Listen, on this ship, we do not steer with a wheel; we use a jog switch. Have you ever used a jog?"

"Yes, sir," I answered.

"Oh you have, have you?" he asked, with a tone that suggested he had caught me lying.

"Yes, sir," I replied.

"Tell me then," he quizzed, "if I were to push the jog this way, what would happen?"

I answered, "You'd activate the rudder to starboard, and the rudder indicator would likewise move to starboard."

Having passed the separating-the-men-from-the-boys test when lashing boxcars, and then properly-securing-the-deck-for-sea test, I was now facing the steering-the-ship-using-a-jog-switch test. He stated the compass heading and invited me to step up onto the steering platform.

The *Wedell Foss*, a beautifully sleek vessel, cut through the sea straight and clean. Having a large compass with exceptionally clear markings, I sensed within moments of taking the jog switch that the ship could (in flat water) be steered to a half degree, if desired. The captain noted my ease and suddenly burst into a multilayered question, all in one breath: "Who are you? Where'd you come from? I've never heard of you."

I answered, "I'm Roy Getman. I'm from Sitka, and worked for Sampson Tug and Barge."

There was a long silence, and then he suddenly burst out with the names, "George and Louie Baggen, Sitka, I should have known. I should have known. I should have known."

Speaking most emphatically, he went on, "I want to tell you something," he said, his lips twisted in angry disgust. "I went to Alaska to earn my fortune. It took me eighteen years to get enough money to get *out* of that place. I vowed I'd *never* be broke again."

From then on, everything between Ed Payne and I was different. The hardness he exhibited in the beginning completely vanished; I was his understanding friend, and in the long of it, I made thirteen round trips between Bellingham and Ward Cove with him.

The vessel's crew was a rigidly subdued lot; the cook printed meal items on a chalkboard, and the men ate in silence.

The tug was based in Bellingham, so at the end of each trip, everyone would go home. Some of the guys lived there. Others of us lived in Seattle and found it most convenient to commute by passenger train since the terminal at Bellingham was close to where the tug was moored. The train guys, because of the common comradery of workingmen, made sure we Foss fellows were given a private car with the most lavish seats.

The rail barge was kept in its own nearby Louisiana Pacific slip. Meanwhile, loading and unloading boxcars was the job of railroad people. By the time those of us from Seattle arrived, a shunting locomotive would usually have the boxcars on the barge.

As soon as we had our personal gear on board and were dressed for work, the tug would maneuver into position and lashing boxcars would then begin. By "lashing" I'm talking about putting jacks under all four corners of each boxcar, and four opposing turnbuckles to eliminate even slightest possible movement of boxcars while making the trip.

Those jacks and turnbuckles were heavy, putting an awful strain on an already bad back. Dragging them into place and then lifting and tightening each one truly did "separate the men from the boys." Regulations governing workmen would likely not allow such heavy work today.

Northbound trips were made carrying empty boxcars. The empties would then be exchanged with loaded ones at Ward Cove—loaded with bundles of partially processed paper to be delivered to Louisiana Pacific in Bellingham.

There was always the span of time it took to off-load empty boxcars and reload the barge with full ones. Waiting, depending on watch times and tide height, gave opportunity to get off the tug and walk ashore.

On one particularly pleasant day, I went ashore to enjoy the fresh aromas of spring and walk the trail beside the pipeline that fed water to the mill. Perhaps a third of a mile along, I came upon a bright young lady sitting on a stump, dangling her feet over its edge. "Hi," I said. "What's your name?"

"Faith," she replied.

She was from the States and in Alaska to visit friends. When her friends went to work, she had nothing to do, and they dropped her off so that she could go for a walk. She knew nothing about the area.

"Do you want to walk with me?" I asked.

"Yes," she readily agreed.

We walked the distance to and from the lake, and still having time before loading, I brought her to the tug to meet the fellows. Her colorful spark and youthful curiosity aroused delightful smiles on these otherwise stoic-faced men. I accompanied her to the place where she had been dropped off in good time to be picked up by her friends.

Spring, summer, fall, and winter trips were more or less repetitive. After lashing boxcars at Ward Cove, the tug and barge would leave for Bellingham. When clear of Mountain Point Ketchikan, the engine would be brought up to rpm and continue without change day and night for the next sixty hours—six hundred nautical miles.

The *Wedell Foss* was a good vessel, and greatly reliable in all weathers—the steady throb of its big engine always comforting.

One time, while the tug was making its way south, and while I was off watch, I ascended the stairs to the bridge and opened the door. Chief Mate John Swisher, a lean, raw-boned fellow, was attending the bridge and his sailor was steering. John, from his station on the port side of the pilothouse, stared at me with a questioning look.

I asked, "Permission to enter the bridge, sir?"

After hesitating a moment, he answered, "Permission granted."

With that, I took the seat on the starboard side and said nothing for perhaps an hour, then stood and asked, "Permission to leave the bridge, sir?"

"Permission granted," he answered with a questioning look on his face. I left quietly and closed the door securely.

On another occasion, ocean waves were running high in Milbanke Sound. I was off watch when called by the captain, who said there was a problem. He asked if I would be willing to go aboard the barge with the mate, explaining that a string of boxcars had broken loose and were moving dangerously about on the barge.

Just getting the tug alongside the barge in those conditions would be difficult, and leaping from tug to barge would be dicey; then bringing the loaded boxcars under control and lashing them again in *those* conditions seemed impossible, but... *Hey,* I thought, *why say "impossible" before trying.*

The captain assured me that he could not order a man to risk his life; he would fully understand if I had hesitation. Considering the captain's good ability with the tug, and the mate's nimbleness—although in his sixties, he moved like a fellow in his twenties—of course, I agreed.

The tug was rising and falling in the swells, and the barge was rolling. Together and well timed, John and I leapt to the deck of the barge and scampered to grab something solid. Working swiftly and without words, we managed to secure the boxcars and get safely back on the tug.

John was openly communicative after that, and even had a sense of humor. He'd sometimes cleverly erase a letter or two on the galley chalkboard, which would cause the menu to read in a comical way. Such was the beginning of laughter and conversation among the fellows. Even the cook, who had previously isolated himself, began to join in.

Home was the ketch *Ivanhoe* at Salmon Bay Marina, and I had precious days with Rachel and the boys between trips on *Wedell Foss*. One sunny day, a big Cadillac pulled up with the captain and his wife, a little round-faced lady with soft, trusting eyes. She looked like a captain's wife. They had brought a watermelon, which has no particular meaning today, but to people like Captain Ed Payne, who lived and struggled in yesteryear's fruitless Alaska, I most certainly understood the significance of this humble gift.

One day while at sea and on watch, the captain seemed troubled, so I encouraged him to talk. At first, he said he was afraid that his words would hurt me. I urged him again, and finally he said, "You're the best sailor I've ever had" and then added, "by far." I listened carefully. The sum of what he was advising was that I not "waste" my life on tugs.

Hurt? His words *did* hurt. Waste? I don't think so. I'd done my best; the sea and these kinds of men were my world, and he was advising me to leave it, and them.

Family of Six

LIFE CONTINUED ON *Ivanhoe* at Salmon Bay Marina. Rachel felt that it was important for us to have a pet after she saw the boys cruelly teasing a duck. She said that they needed to learn about kindness to animals. I had no objection. Except for Victor the seal, I had never lived close to an animal.

She went looking and soon came home with a cute grey kitten with white feet. We named her Bootsie, and she quickly won all our hearts as we watched her many playful antics.

Then one day, little more than a year later, I stepped inside *Ivanhoe* after an errand and noted her little collar on my bunk. Rachel said that Bootsie had been run over in the parking space beside the boat.

It happened at a time on the calendar when it was my turn to go on (by then) the ship-handling tug *Carol Foss*.

Losing Bootsie was much more troubling than could have been imagined; I tried to tell myself that she was only an animal. Self-talk might have convinced me, *if* she had been an *outside* cat, but no, she was one with us and usually pitched in helping Paul and Jim when they built things using Lego toys.

I contacted Rachel from the pay phone at Pier 28 and asked her to look for another grey cat. On a later call, she said she had found one at a pet place in Lynnwood and assured me that the cat she found looked a lot like Bootsie, but with a shorter tail. She went on to say that there were other cats, but this one, rather than being caged like the others, had been allowed to run free; she was sure I would like it.

After my fifteen-day stint on the tug, I returned to *Ivanhoe*, stepped inside with my sea bag, and was soon looking into the undeviatingly bright eyes of a fully-grown shorthaired Russian Blue. Those eyes studied me intensely from the vantage of what had already become *her* place on the starboard bunk. To her, I was the newcomer. After perhaps a full minute, those discerning eyes suddenly softened in a way that conveyed my acceptance.

We named her Dusty, because she seemed to be dusted with silver.

One day, I came up out of *Ivanhoe* and saw a lady sitting on a chair between parked vehicles, close to the side of *Ivanhoe*, with an easel and canvas directly in front of her. She held a brush in her right hand and a painter's pallet with blobs of various colors in her left.

The lady would have made a good subject for a painting herself, dressed as she was in a quaint summer dress. The only distraction was that she was seated in a limited space between two parked cars.

She saw my interest, and after a few casual words, invited me to come around where I could see the light pencil lines she had drawn on the canvas. I noted that she'd begun her colorful brush strokes.

Neither she nor I noticed Dusty until she leapt from one car and landed on the palette in the lady's left hand in a posture ready to leap again to the shiny black Lincoln on our left. I grabbed the cat in midair and saved the happening.

Each of Dusty's four dainty paws was a different color.

The lady wasn't amused.

Our good friends were John and Jeane Story, who came to visit on *Ivanhoe* quite often. One day, Jeane brought us a grey kitten with a white bib and lovely markings around his eyes, saying we needed another cat so that Dusty would have company.

We named the little guy Buster. Strangely, Dusty ignored the kitten until we purposely made a fuss over him, and then she did as well. She began teaching him everything he needed to know about being a cat and living on a boat. All this is important, because now it was Rachel and me, Paul and Jim, and Dusty and Buster, making us a family of six.

Vocabulary Vacuum

As I'VE SAID, John and Jeane were special friends and visited us on *Ivanhoe* often. On one of those visits, Jeane—well-groomed, well-educated, well-read, and attractive—talked about intelligence. She explained that intelligence is directly related to vocabulary, and told me that I had a very small one.

She was right about my limited vocabulary, but linking it to intelligence was even more of an insult. I knew that vocabulary came from reading, a good education, and from being around others with language skills, but that wasn't my world nor the opportunities I'd had in life.

Besides, I had a reading problem—it helped to use a ruler to keep my place on a page. Even so, I was able to study and learn, not because it was easy but because of interest and determination. Even before my teens, I was into my father's many mechanical and electrical manuals. Being so immersed in his world from early on may have been a disadvantage in some ways, but overall, mine was a big and full upbringing and what Jeane said was cruel and really hurt me. Maybe I *was* educationally lopsided.

Speaking about reading, Rachel and I had a stretch of relaxing days away from everything when we could enjoy doing nothing. Rachel buried herself in historical novels, and I studied Sperry Vickers *Industrial Hydraulics Manual*. I recommend reading things like hydraulics manuals to your children or grand-children when tucking them in. It will put them to sleep faster than any of the traditional bedtime stories such as *Goldie Bear and the Three Locks*.

While still suffering the pain of Jeane's comments, Foss wanted me on a tug in Cook Inlet, Alaska. Goodbye, Jeane, and hello, Diane—*Diane Foss*, that is.

I joined the seventy-two-foot-long steel tug *Diane Foss* at Kenai, just as the ice was breaking up. That was March 1967. I noted a book on the shelf when going down the companionway to my quarters. Its title revealed that it taught vocabulary, so I placed it with my stuff in the stateroom and over the next ninety days, studied it cover to cover.

That book not only taught vocabulary but also had a clever way of introducing and explaining words, later reinforcing them in a way that secondarily taught how to teach. It didn't turn me into a voluminous reader, but it did help to build my vocabulary.

The cook on *Diane Foss* was a gracious man, around sixty years old, by the name Clay. He had a gifted command of English and a gainful grasp of humor. Noting my thirst for learning, he began teaching the power of communication. His personal tutorage went on for the duration of my time aboard.

God had to be watching. There I was, suffering crushed feelings in Seattle, and days later, I had a book on vocabulary in my stateroom and a private tutor in the galley—in Cook Inlet, the last place on earth one might expect to gain language skills.

Blip on Radar

RED HENDERSHOT WAS operator of a fifty-six-foot-long landing craft working in proximity with *Diane Foss* in Cook Inlet. Several oil drill rigs had been set into the ocean floor north of our location. Oil from each was pumped to a pipeline that ran down the inlet to a sizable tank farm near us—a place called Drift River, where there were construction workers, some buildings, and a gravel airstrip.

Diane Foss was there to tend floating equipment involved in the building of an offshore terminal for loading supertankers. Red's landing craft was there to move men and things between various pieces of floating equipment and also men and equipment to and from the shore. A gigantic floating derrick served as moorage for the tug, as well as the landing craft.

Cook Inlet has the greatest tides in the world, second only to the Bay of Fundy. Enormous current activity takes place as a result of the exchange of water in and out of the inlet twice a day. Timing to get a landing craft on or off the shore had to be carefully executed. The maneuver was often done in poor weather, sometimes in darkness, and sometimes in drift ice.

Cook Inlet has no real beaches. Soupy brown mud fills the expanse between high and low tide. Grassy weeds gradually merge with brush and deciduous trees extending up the slopes, culminating at Mount Redoubt, a steaming volcano just above our location.

We on the *Diane Foss* crew stayed on the tug, which meant we had everything with us. I could grab a needed jacket or gloves, or a cup of coffee when desired, but the rest of the floating workforce, including Red, were housed inside the floating derrick. It was held in place by cables reaching out in six directions to six ten-ton anchors on the seabed. Those who lived inside this

Herculean giant had what they needed, and all went to their stations to work every day, but when Red went to his landing craft, he had no comfort. Much of his work had to be timed for high tide or slack current, and he would sometimes miss supper or be out working when others were resting.

His landing craft was typical, having three main parts: an area in the bow to carry things, a compartment in the stern for two noisy and smoky GM (Jimmy) diesels, and an operator's console housed in a small pilothouse. Heat from the two engines kept his post relatively warm. Red also had a portable AC household-type electric heater that he could plug in when the landing craft was tied to the side of the big floating derrick.

One night, Red and his craft left the side of the derrick to pick up some equipment from the shore at high water. Everything was loaded as planned. The landing craft backed away from the shore then swung around for the return, but in the black of night, it became mired, and by then, Red was alone and the tide was dropping. Without seawater for cooling, the engines had to be stopped. Being resourceful, he started up a big diesel-welding machine that had just come aboard. This machine was designed to make DC current for welding. He ran a cord to it and plugged the heater in. Its fan, intended for AC household current, burst into flames. Some water still surrounded the craft; using the electric heater's own cord, he lowered it into the sea to put the fire out. He hauled it back and plugged it in again. He said it glowed red and kept the pilothouse warm, but the fan never worked again.

A radio was installed in the landing craft after that.

No matter how much sleep Red missed, he was always at his station during the workday, but like any construction job, he would sometimes have nothing to do but wait. I used such times, on occasion, to take some goodie or hot chocolate to him. Red was a red-haired, muscular hulk of a man who had a perpetual mean and angry look. It was difficult to interpret his response to those kindnesses.

One day, I noticed Red had a pile of wrenches on the deck beside the hatch to the engine compartment. He emerged, wiped his forehead, exchanged some tools, and went back down. It happened a second time; being curious, I went over and asked him what he was working on and offered to help. He gestured for me to climb into the engine compartment. It took time to adjust to the dismal lighting. We crawled to the back of the compartment behind the engines. There, Red had built a bed. "The rag and tools," he explained, "are just to make it look like work."

In the scheme of constructions, a new barge was brought in and secured to a substantial pylon near the shore. Red was to use the landing craft at high water to bring it out to the derrick.

This time, he took another man with him.

It was absolutely black outside when Red was getting ready to leave. Since he now had a radio, I said I would track the landing craft on radar and guide him to the barge near the shore, which I'd also be able to see on radar. Seeing his way back to the derrick would be no concern for Red, as lights on the tug and derrick would guide his way.

Red and his man motored out into the dark of night. Those engines idled poorly. Instead of a smooth sounding *little little little little little little*, they hunted with an obnoxious *bro wrap bro wrap bro wrap bro wrap* noise.

I heard the engines speed up some. Since Red was wandering off in an uncertain southerly direction, I picked up the hand-held microphone and asked what course he was steering.

He answered, "I don't know."

So I asked again, and again, the answer was, "I don't know."

Then he explained that the engine vibration made the compass card go round and round in circles. I told him, "Stick your right arm out and point right. That is the direction you need to go."

Radar showed the landing craft making an uncertain arc toward the west. I got on the radio again and said, "You've got the right idea, Red, but you need to come around some more."

Over the next while, I stood in the pilothouse of the tug, holding the microphone and watching the radar screen while guiding Red's radar blip toward the new barge's radar blip.

"Red, you've got to slow down," I said, and heard the engines come down to their ragged *bro wrap bro wrap bro wrap* as a response. "Red, can you see the barge?"

"No," he said. "I can't see *anything!*"

It didn't help that the new barge was painted jet black.

The *bro wrap bro wrap bro wrap* sound of those engines continued across the water, then there was a distinct change as the engines could be heard going into neutral and reverse with an enormous *ROARRRRRR* of throttle. Why was Red backing those engines? Just then, there was a great *CLAANGGGGGGG*. Everything went silent. After a long time, Red came on the radio and said, "We found it."

Being in the black of night, Red had his man up on the bow ramp looking ahead. When they realized the stout landing craft could collide sharply with the steel barge, he put the engines in hard reverse, thinking to stop all forward momentum. Neither man realized that the landing craft had already passed the barge, nor did they sense the great burst of throttle in reverse had them moving backward at a considerable rate. While both gazed forward into the blackness, the landing craft had backed squarely into the side of the barge.

THE DAY CAME, eighty-seven days after my arrival in Cook Inlet, when I was to leave the tug, catch a company air flight to Anchorage, and then home. My ride to shore was in the landing craft with Red. There I said goodbye. There was no detectable expression on his face as he muttered an acknowledgement.

I continued on tugs in Puget Sound for the next years and kept alert for news regarding Red. Most reports were sketchy. Somebody said he was on a big tug "way up north," which I assumed to mean Alaska's North Slope.

I left working on Foss tugs and settled on Vancouver Island in 1969. That was the end of any connection with Red Hendershot.

Now, jumping ahead to tell the rest of story about Red— In 1980, I was operating the mission vessel *Coastal Messenger,* and that summer, we brought the vessel in through the Ballard locks and tied at Fisherman's Terminal. Coming out a few days later, we went into the locks and tied on the right side behind a thirty-some-foot sailboat. An old powerboat motored in with a repugnant *brupp brupp brupp* exhaust sound and was directed to move all the way up on the left side.

One at a time, the locks filled with sailboats of various shapes and sizes, and then the great steel doors closed. By now, every engine was silent. It was a pleasantly warm day. People on sailboats stood on decks, watching as the water level began to drop.

A massive figure slowly emerged from the rear cabin door of the old cruiser, and like an Alaska brown bear, made his way to the stern and planted paws far apart on the waist-high transom. With his head weaving from side to side, he surveyed the many sailboats and people astern.

It was Red! I stepped out on deck and hailed across, "Hendershot! I'd recognize that face anywhere!"

He obviously recognized me and answered in a voice as deep as ever, yet with a tinge of patriarchal warmth. "Oh… Hi…" he said with a trailing sound, like a whale exhaling a mass of air.

The walls of the locks amplified his meaty tones.

"What kind of work are you doing these days?" I asked.

"Tug… Bering Sea," he said, with his voice resounding off the walls.

I repeated his words as a question: "Bering Sea?"

"Yup," he answered.

People on sailboats began turning to listen.

"Yup," Red repeated.

Quizzically, I continued, "What do you like about *that* part of the world?"

Red hesitated for a moment, furled his brow, and answered with some amplification, "No police! No rules!"

By now, eyes from every nimble and handsome man and every lovely woman in colorful yachting apparel were fixed on Red. He slowly sucked in his breath, doubled both fists, lifted a defiant jaw, and with eyes now aflame, irritably scanned every face. Then, in a powerful bass voice, boomed out the words, "AND NO SAILBOATS!"

Ship's Clock

GETTING BACK TO my time on tugs—there's more to tell. After those ninety days in Cook Inlet on the tug *Diane Foss*, I was assigned to the tug *Carol Foss,* which primarily assisted ships in and out of Puget Sound ports—mainly Seattle.

In this case, our crew came aboard at noon on the fifteenth of each month and went home on the last day of the month (we always had the extra day on months having thirty-one days).

This went on for close to two years, and then in May 1969, I went to the Foss office and asked to take the full summer off to enjoy family cruising with *Ivanhoe.* Blessing was given with assurance that I would *always* have a place with Foss.

After coming off that month's stint on *Carol Foss*, Rachel and I, Paul and Jim, and cats Dusty and Buster were off to the biggest and best thing that could ever happen to any family—sailing, cruising, hiking, exploring places, and enjoying beaches and each other.

We eventually came into Sidney on Vancouver Island and reported into Canada Customs. Rachel and I told the officer we had two sons and two cats. With a Scottish accent, the kindly officer, said, "We don't bother much about cots."

Oh, if only our precious *Ivanhoe* could talk. From that day, she was back in her own familiar waters, where she had frolicked under young billowing sails.

Former owner, Ralph Vittery, had told us *Ivanhoe's* history when we bought it. Built in Vancouver in 1906, it was intended to be a personal yacht for the shipyard's owner but was soon sold to somebody for the staggering sum of (we laugh now) eight hundred and seventy-five dollars. The craft started life as a gaff-rigged sloop but was re-masted in the late thirties and re-rigged as a Marconi ketch.

Ralph talked about a Major Jukes who owned *Ivanhoe* for many years and was financially able to keep the craft in top condition. Ralph and Bea bought it in the early fifties, and Ralph (being a shipwright) kept it in finest condition.

Our having *Ivanhoe* again in British Columbia waters caused the names Vittery and Jukes to come up from time to time as we moved around and met different people. We knew it had been a difficult decision for Ralph and Bea to sell *Ivanhoe*, but it was never clear why Ralph wanted to keep the clock. The spot on the bulkhead where it had been removed was a slightly brighter shade of wood.

We were in Maple Bay when I turned to Rachel and asked, "I wonder what it would take to stay in Canada and put our boys in school." Days later, we walked into the Office of Immigration in Nanaimo and asked the attending officer the same thing. The man pulled out a form and filled it in. The process took perhaps forty minutes. One space asked how we had gotten to Canada, and he penned in the words, "Sailing Ship *Ivanhoe*."

We had kept in loose contact with Ralph, but when we knew we'd be staying in British Columbia, we went to North Vancouver to visit face to face.

Ralph asked Rachel, "What was the date when *Ivanhoe* came back into Canada?"

She hesitated a few moments, then said "July 7, 1969."

"I wondered," Ralph said, and then told a most unusual story about the ship's clock. "I removed the clock from *Ivanhoe* and brought it home," he said. "For some reason, it no longer worked, so I took it to a repair shop, and after careful examination, the clock smith said that the mainspring was ruined and told me, 'Take your clock home, Ralph, and put it up where you can enjoy the memory; it cannot be fixed.'"

So that is what Ralph did. One day, he heard the sound of its bell in the living room, and to his astonishment, the clock was going again and continued to run just fine from then on. He noted the day: July 7, 1969.

Shipyard Pink

SEPTEMBER WAS COMING, and we knew we'd be wintering in Nanaimo, so I talked to Jack Weeks, owner of the Anchorage Marina about moorage for our *Ivanhoe*. He assigned a snug place handy to the gangway and parking ashore. Our new family address was 1520 Stewart Avenue, Nanaimo.

Using public transportation, we retrieved our car from Seattle. Matters for legal entrance into Canada were easy then. The car, *Ivanhoe,* and everything we owned were listed as household goods.

The boys started school at Princess Anne in September, and immigration paperwork came through on the eighteenth. It was obviously time to think about finding a job.

I pulled out my boat carpentry tools and sharpened the chisels in preparation of going to work. Understanding the importance of first impressions, I dressed nicely and walked the short distance to Nanaimo Shipyard where I met its superintendent, Robert Simpson, a composed and rather stiff former military person.

He began the job interview. It reminded me of an old war movie in which the officer dresses down the enlisted man. Part of his approach was to fire questions faster than could be answered.

Seeing clearly into his game, I quietly stood and turned to leave. "Oh," he said, with a sudden change of demeanor, "you can go to work at eight in the morning."

I arrived at the jobsite before eight the next morning, seriously wondering what sort of fellows I'd be working with when I saw some bad words, including the F word, painted on the side of a shed but spelled wrong.

Superintendent Robert Simpson met me on the lower grounds. We watched a newly constructed sailboat of about thirty-four feet being hauled out of the water. He pointed out that there was no clear demarcation of its waterline and asked me to figure out where it should be.

It seemed a strange assignment to be put on such a job on one's first day, especially when I *thought* I was hired to be a boat carpenter. But so what? One part of life prepares for another; that was the case with my earlier boat shop in Sitka and a lot of other things. I knew how to do the job and did it. White hull, red bottom, and a nice boot stripe all around. When launched, the boat's owner was pleased, Robert Simpson was happy, and my first paycheck was at the top journeyman rate.

I was seldom called on for carpentry—maybe because the superintendent heard me say I could read blueprints. Some months later, he talked to me about designing a tug. His idea for its shape was unconventional, but I listened closely and did my best to turn his abstract ideas into a tangible design: thirty-three feet long, eleven feet wide, and six feet deep. The shipyard went to work on the various parts over the next while, and when finished, it was launched with the name *NS 101*. It apparently worked well. I saw it from time to time over the next twenty-some years, working with logs in Ladysmith Harbour.

The shipyard had recently lost their regular painter due to failing health. Perhaps it was the waterline paint job on the new sailboat that sparked the assumption I was the new shipyard painter.

Large shipyard contracts included annual maintenance on many of the Department of Highway ferries that served communities and islands along the lower British Columbia coast. My part, using several men to assist, was to attend to safety equipment and all aspects of painting.

Without permission, I began to modernize color schemes of each ferry that came in. Old glum government green was changed to happy white. Black decks in passenger areas were changed to porch and floor green. The old Spar Buff, a pumpkin color, was popular as a sort of wainscoting on fish cannery vessels, tugs, and bigger workboats going back to the 1930s. I did away with that old style completely. Passenger spaces and superstructures became white.

Somebody must have noticed, because at some point, a directive came to the shipyard from somewhere. It insisted that all Department of Highway ferries were to henceforth conform to the prescribed scheme. Going through attached pages revealed that the "new" conformity matched what I had taken the freedom to modernize.

Peak periods of work at the shipyard called for using extra persons from Canada Manpower. It was assumed that I was to break them in—no easy task, since some were new to the world of work, and that included Grubby.

The ferry *Westwood* was in for its annual everything, so after getting a team on varnishing wooden seats in the passenger lounge, I gave Grubby the job of painting pipes connecting hot water radiators in that same area.

I was then off to other parts of the vessel, and minutes later, someone from the varnish team rushed up and said, "Grubby is ruining the varnish."

"He's not on varnish," I said.

The fellow insisted that I follow him quickly. Grubby was happily slapping the paint brush up and down on a pipe, an action that was sending droplets of green through the air and onto the wet varnish.

I was very kind to Grubby, explained what had gone wrong, and said, "Just leave your paint and brush and follow me." I took him to work with the "black" crew. They had already prepared the car deck and were ready to start the painting using long-handled rollers. Being just one color, and working with others, there was little concern for drips, smudges, or smears.

Several gallons of black had been poured into a five-gallon pail. A measure of thinner had been added. "Be sure to stir it well," I emphasized.

Meanwhile, the "white" crew had set up scaffolding and was applying paint to structures above the car deck.

Minutes later, I was urgently summoned with the words, "Grubby is ruining everything!" I soon learned that he had stirred the black so vigorously that it had been slung upward and gotten on the white.

So again, I told Grubby I had another job for him.

There was a flush hatch on the foredeck of the ferry that gave access to the forepeak. All surfaces in that utilitarian compartment were one color: aluminum. I went over the job carefully to be sure Grubby understood what was to be done.

Less than an hour later, several guys came running up shouting, "Grubby is out!" He was standing on the foredeck, completely aluminum coloured, except for his eyes. Two fellows, one on each side, were keeping him from venturing beyond the round hole in the deck.

"How's your painting coming?" I asked.

"I'm done," he answered.

"You were fast. Did you paint *everything?*"

He nodded.

"You are all aluminum," I said.

"I fell down," he replied.

I put him next on steam cleaning with another guy in the greatly soiled engine room of a boat that had sunk.

CHANGING SUBJECTS, WE had a way of cleaning whole engine compartments. Floorboards were removed and prepared and painted separately. Planks were laid as temporary surfaces to walk on. Portable floodlights were set up to make everything highly visible. Anything sensitive to water and cleaners was prepared and painted separately, and when dry, were covered with plastic and carefully masked.

Spray equipment was used to spread cleaning solutions throughout the compartment, then pressured water was used to wash every surface until all was squeaky-clean. Heaters and fans were used to speed drying. The full process took days.

I always did the final spray painting inside compartments. As for breathing, I had a paint suit with a hood connected to piped-in air that vented outward through the face part.

It was my discipline to always first apply a white primer coat. Since the next and finish coat in any engine space would be gloss marine white, the under-coat was always tinted slightly to give a distinction between the two whites.

In one case of undercoating a rather large engine compartment, I was ready with four gallons of white primer and nearly ready to begin spraying. First, however, I needed to tint it. Seeing a can of Signal Red nearby, I stirred in a small amount.

Only after painting the entire compartment did I realize how passionately pink this coat of primer looked in the brilliance of floodlights, but who cared? All would be covered by the final coating of gloss white.

Just then, someone's foot pushed the unlatched watertight entry door open. It was shipyard mechanic, Howard Johnson, a thin fellow with a shallow chest and small round potbelly. He was clutching a tool tray with both hands and had a bent cigarette in his mouth. Seeing the engine room brightly lit in bright pink, his mouth dropped open. The cigarette fell out. He stood blinking.

"Oh, Howard," I asked nonchalantly, "tell me what you think of this light shade of gray." His lips moved as he tried to speak, but no words came out.

First Years In Nanaimo

OVER THE NEXT while, home was *Ivanhoe* at Anchorage Marina.

The boys would leave for school wearing floatation vests, and hang them on a nail on the wall outside the outboard shop. Once in a while, they'd forget and wear them all the way to Princess Anne.

The cats loved playing on the floats, and in time took possession. Dusty, the female, always took the lead. One day, they trapped a big dog out on the end of a finger float. When the dog realized what was happening, his expression suddenly went from slobber face to fire-breathing dragon. The dog's owner saw what was happening and quickly rescued the situation.

Rachel talked about finding a church. I was busy seven days a week at the shipyard but readily agreed, saying, "Especially if it has a good Sunday school for the boys."

We knew nothing about Nanaimo's churches, and I left finding one to Rachel. Being long before Google, she looked in a phone book and found one listed on Departure Bay Road. She and the boys attended that next Sunday, and I was happy for them.

By then into fall 1969, two commercial fish boats, *Full Moon* and *Silver Tide*, came in and moored close to *Ivanhoe*, captained by Ken Singer and Ray Sorheim. Both had homes ashore but were often on their boats or on the float when I came home from work.

One day, they told me that two well-dressed ladies had been on *Ivanhoe*.

Strange, I thought, *I don't know any ladies in Canada.* I carried on to *Ivanhoe*, and Rachel greeted me happily and said two ladies from the church had visited.

Two weeks later, Ken and Ray again stopped me, saying a man wearing a suit had come to *Ivanhoe*. Not connecting the man's visit with the women, I wondered if he was someone from Immigration, but when I stepped aboard, Rachel said the pastor of the church had come by. Again, I was pleased.

Demands at the shipyard tapered off in the autumn, allowing opportunity to go to church and meet the people. (I'll say more about that in the next chapter).

I had built a dingy that could be easily launched from its cradle on *Ivanhoe*. One Saturday, I had the boys and Buster the cat out for a row. Paul and Jim were sitting on seats, and Buster was balancing with his paws in a straight line on the narrow edge of the plywood transom. Each time I took an oar stroke, Buster would shift his weight, as only a cat is able to do.

Rachel, watching from the deck of *Ivanhoe,* called out, "Buster is going to fall in the water!" Hearing his name, he jumped in and happily swam to her.

NEWCASTLE ISLAND, A lovely forested park, was directly across a narrow channel from the Marina. We'd often row over, pull the boat up onto the grass, and go hiking on the island's many trails.

The boys fit well in every area of life and often had visiting friends. By 1971, it was obvious that we had outgrown *Ivanhoe,* so we moved ashore, cats and all, and our cherished old *Ivanhoe* was sold to a fifth owner—another Ralph— this time Ralph Yontez.

Mysterious Prompt

OUR FIRST MOVING ashore in Nanaimo was to a temporary rental house that had a wolf-hide throw rug in the living room, complete with a realistic head with eyes and teeth. It was very dead, but the cats killed it a lot more. We later moved into a nice duplex on Beaufort Crescent, where we lived for the next many years.

Leaving Nanaimo Shipyard in May 1972 and going to work on the tug *Lawrence L* out of North Vancouver was a big step for me. The tugs schedule of two weeks on and two weeks off gave the needed breakaway from the shipyard's taxing demands.

Rachel was by then working in the office at Malaspina College, and our boys were in school. Even though I was away half the time on the tug, I had considerably more time for family and friends, and time to be happily involved with what had become our Departure Bay church family.

Dave Thompson was a true pastor and an excellent Bible teacher. My only complaint, if one might call it a complaint, was that he sometimes used theological terms beyond common understanding. I spoke to him about it, because I didn't want to miss anything.

Rachel and I and several others were sitting a few rows back from the pulpit one Sunday when he used one of those big words. I quietly said, in humor, "I used to have one of those but had it removed."

Those nearby chuckled. Pastor Dave looked down, hesitated briefly, and then said, "Let me rephrase that."

Dave's good wife, Miriam, a quiet-spirited person and powerful support, was often the pianist for church services and for the choir, which I thoroughly enjoyed being part of on every possible occasion.

When not away on the tug, I could drive Rachel to work at the college then have use of the car, which gave me the freedom to venture down to the harbour. Having worked at the shipyard, and on tugs, and being generally oriented to things on the waterfront, I was able to relate to most anyone and any happening. Being two years on the ship-handling tug, *Carol Foss*, in Puget Sound, I also knew the protocol for going aboard the different ships coming into Nanaimo's harbour. Using English as a common language and having an ability to draw, I could communicate easily.

I didn't realize I was being a missionary.

I was home on days off the tug one day in May 1972, when I opened the door and started across the living room. Rachel was at the college and the boys were in school. A thought crossed my mind: *Contact the Shantymen*. Such a thought was so isolated, so abrupt, so out of place from anything I'd been thinking, that I stopped and stood, wondering what could have triggered it.

I remembered the Shantymen. Nice guys, they and their vessel *Messenger III* came to our village in Alaska in the early 1950s. I wondered if that group was still in existence.

Few readers will know what I'm talking about. To explain, a shanty is a logger's shack. A man by the name William Henderson began carrying the gospel to loggers that lived in shanties in remote northern Ontario in 1906. Over time, his type of work expanded, and Vancouver Island had a branch of Shantymen dating back to the early 1930s. I went to the phone book to look for a number without success.

I phoned a man, someone Rachel had done some secretarial work for, by the name of Walter Heindrichs, a well-ordered person living in Nanaimo. I had noted that he knew a lot about churches and missionary organizations.

Our conversation was brief:

"Do you have a contact number for the Shantymen?"

He had the information in less than a minute. "Don Robertson," he said, and gave me a phone number and address in Victoria.

Having the information so quickly and easily after that unexpected thought had me wondering if it were something providential, or merely something that had popped into my head. My first thought was to ignore it, but if it were something from the Lord, I knew I'd better not.

I said little to Rachel about it, other than that we needed to treat our upcoming Saturday as a family outing to Victoria, and that I wanted to meet a fellow there. I decided not to phone ahead but to treat the thing as a test. If the man were home, I would see it as a possible divine prompt. If not, I'd drop the matter.

After touring the city's lovely waterfront, we found the address.

Rachel and the boys remained in the car while I got out and walked to the entrance of a rather large apartment complex. The name "Robertson" was on the number pad, and I pressed the button. A deep voice answered.

"I'm Roy Getman," I said. "I'm here to meet Don Robertson."

"Come right in," the voice replied.

I stepped into the lobby as a large, slow-moving figure emerged out a door into the hallway. When we were face to face, I asked, "Don Robertson?" He nodded affirmatively.

Concluding by then that my unusual prompt had to be providential, I said, "I came to inquire about working with the Shantymen."

He showed no surprise and asked where I lived. I told him. He said that he and his wife had visitors in from Australia and wondered if he could come and see me in Nanaimo on Monday.

He arrived as expected.

I was curious about the present work of the Shantymen and told him how I remembered the vessel *Messenger III* from the early 1950s. He said that those involved with the vessel had grown old and *Messenger III* had been sold.

As we talked, I realized that what I'd been doing on my own was not unlike what Shantymen missionaries did in different settings across Canada.

News of my interest reached the ears of the few dozen persons who were involved in monthly meetings of the Vancouver Island branch. They concluded that mine was a "call."

Missionary First Months

DON TOOK ME around to meet people over a wide area during the weeks that followed. He also talked about plans for the summer, saying that my first involvement would be to conduct children's programs in mostly remote communities on Vancouver Island.

Children's programs? He must have read my face, quickly adding that I'd have plenty of help. He also said I'd be given use of the Shantymen truck and camper.

I was surprised at its neglect when seeing it a few days later. Its fiberglass camper had a bashed-in back corner, and its sides were seriously marred by limb scratches. Its interior was dirty and uncared for, with broken hinges, loose trim, and missing knobs and handles.

Being a boat-repair guy, I fixed everything and refinished it so it was as good as new. Don was delighted. The cost was one hundred twenty-seven dollars and a few cents from my own pocket. I presented the receipts through channels as instructed by Don.

Some days later, the matter of my "careless" spending came up as a criticism in a meeting. Had I known, I would not have submitted the receipts for reimbursement.

The first children's gathering was in the small logging community at Honeymoon Bay. Rachel was off work for the summer by then, and our boys were out of school, making the assignment a fun family thing.

Don Robertson's wife, Elva, played a lively piano, and Don's sixteen-year-old daughter, Joanne, knew the children songs. I simply mirrored her words and actions. Don had also enlisted the help of Joan McKee, who (having been a primary-school teacher) was especially good with children and had a special way of holding everyone's attention. Rachel joined in helping in the background, attending to such things as a little one's tears or dealing as needed with a child's over-active behavior.

I wondered about God's humour, putting a sailor, boat carpenter, shipyard painter, or whatever I was, up in front leading summer programs. Of course, drawing pictures and doing fun things with my *own* kids had always been important. This setting was only an enlargement. To use chalk and illustrate things like Noah and the Ark, Jonah and the whale, or David and Goliath was fun and easy, yet served to hold the attention of young ones. At craft time, I could motivate the least creative child to produce *something* meaningful.

For a child to call me "Mr. Getman" seemed stuffy, and to call me "Roy" seemed inappropriately chummy. Someone came up with "Uncle Roy," and that stuck with the children and the various adults, and continued to stick over the following decades as I came to be known as Uncle Roy up and down the coast. Even my own dear mother sometimes called me "Uncle Roy." Try to explain being an uncle to your own mother.

Earlier, when Rachel and I knew we would be away from home most of that summer, she contacted a real-estate agent to make our home available if needed by someone. The timing was perfect for Pip and Kay, a couple from England needing a place to live while Pip was involved with an engineering project. They gladly took over our home, including looking after our cats, Dusty and Buster.

At one point, we came home to visit Pip and Kay and our cats. The cats were happy to see us but also obviously comfortable with Pip and Kay. Somehow, in the handling of details, we had failed to tell Pip and Kay the cats' names or mention that we always kept a glass of fresh drinking water for them in the bathtub.

Pip had named the cats Snuffles (a description of Dusty's snuffled breathing) and Fluff Duff (which described Buster's furry gray coat with white bib). The cats didn't care what they were called, but they *did* insist that a glass of fresh water needed to be placed in the tub each day.

We continued summer work with children in different communities. The biggest group was close to one hundred and forty children, not to mention a number of sit-in parents.

I missed my cue to be up front on one occasion, and by the time I got there, the children were out of control. Not knowing what to do, I picked up a piece of chalk and began drawing a cat on the board. By the time I finished, the room was silent.

Programs for the summer ended in good time for Pip to finish his project. We then moved back into our home and returned the truck and camper to Victoria. Rachel returned to her place at the college, and the boys went back to school.

Before the summer programs, Don had encouraged me to think beyond the towns. "Many can do church work," he said, while emphasizing that I was able to reach out and beyond.

Being ready to continue, I let Don know that I was ready to use the truck and camper again, and he said that it had been sold! He assured me that the matter of me getting around would be taken up at the next meeting.

Meetings were a month apart.

Knowing how the cost of prettying the camper had stirred up some of the money-minded members, I didn't bother waiting. I simply went to the Ford dealer, bought a new Courier pickup, equipped it for off road use, and set about measuring to build a small camper. Materials were purchased and left in the open bed, ready to start the project the following morning.

Our neighbor, a building contractor, was leaving for work just as I was ready to start. Seeing the stuff in the back, he asked what I was going to make. I told him.

A few days later, he came to me and said, "When you told me you were going to build a camper, I figured I'd let you struggle with it a few days and then help you get started, but when I came home from work and saw the thing practically built, I thought to myself, *This guy is no ordinary preacher!*"

Since Shantymen Camp Ross at Pachena Bay was supposedly in my charge, and so far I knew almost nothing about it, I was eager to learn about the place. Almost before the paint on the Courier camper was dry, I drove to Port Alberni, slept overnight in it, and caught the freight boat *Lady Rose* as a foot passenger the next morning.

We arrived at the fishing village of Bamfield around noon. From there, I walked the gravel road to the camp, where I was happily welcomed and given a room. Its three-acre front yard doubled as the northern terminus of the famed

West Coast Trail. The next day, my thirty-third birthday, I set off hiking the twisting trail under a dense canopy of forest and continued six miles to the Pachena Point lightstation.

That hike was only a small sampling of the arduous trek that continued down the coast another forty miles.

On the way back, I took a side trail leading down to a rocky beach. Drift logs, piled high above the tide line, blocked any easy access.

I climbed up and over the confusion and continued along that stretch of rugged coastline. Ocean waves smashed on jagged rocks on my left.

After some distance, I scaled a large outcropping of rock and bushes, then continued along another length of beach. After perhaps a quarter mile, I decided to cut inland directly through the forest and join the main trail again, but in the attempt, became surrounded and disoriented in a dense jungle of tangled brush. The sounds of the sea were muted, and mist was swirling lazily through the air.

I needed to keep my cool. *There must be a way out of this mess.* The slope of the land was not clearly evident, but I did my best, and to my relief, found the beach again and started back. I climbed over the same rocky projection of land and continued in the direction of the trail I had come down.

When less than a hundred yards away, I caught sight of a cougar crouched behind the mess of logs I'd earlier climbed over. Its eyes were fixed on me.

I froze where I stood.

Only the top of its head was showing, its ears pulled down flat, which is not a good communication. The sea was breaking on rocks behind me. I wondered what chance I would have diving in there. Really, what defense does a man ever have against one of those big powerful cats in any situation? I continued holding absolutely still, not once turning my head or eyes.

The big cat was doing the same with me.

· Cougars can be aggressive, but they can also be shy. After several minutes and having no alternative, I began to advance. The cougar didn't flinch. When within perhaps twenty-five yards, I began wondering if this was just the sea-sculpted end of a golden-brown log amongst weathered grey ones. It took nerve to climb up and confirm that this was indeed the case.

I was back at the lodge before supper.

Beyond the Pier

I RETURNED HOME and completed last details on the camper unit on the Courier, then set out to familiarize myself with Vancouver Island while visiting specific contacts in different places.

Knowing how to get around on Vancouver Island's back roads was mostly by word of mouth. The able little camper was handy. I could stop and take a break, make a cup of coffee or a meal, take a rest, and sleep comfortably overnight.

Public roads ended halfway up the island and then continued again farther up. The way to get from the lower portion to the upper was to take a ferry, locally known as *Turtle Princess*. It ran from Kelsey Bay to Beaver Cove. Dreadfully slow at best, it was even slower when tidal currents opposed.

Another way to get from the lower island to the upper was to drive to Campbell River, cross over to Gold River, and get on logging roads after work hours. In this case, you had to know what you were doing. This was an arduous drive on roads locally referred to as the Ho Chi Minh Trail.

The possibility of a mechanical problem along this lonely and tortuous route was a true concern, especially in the dark of night.

One day, I parked at the head of Muchalat Inlet, not far from Gold River, and walked to the end of the pier. Gazing out over the expanse, I thought about how helpless I felt using a wheeled vehicle on such limited roads when there was a whole coast out there and no means to visit the isolated pockets of people.

I tried to tell myself not to dream about what didn't exist. The Shantymen had sold *Messenger III*; there was no longer the team to give life to an on-going mission vessel. Feeling helpless and not knowing what to pray for, I walked back to the camper, telling myself to realistically consider what I could do alone.

I pulled out a tablet and sketched a seventeen-foot-long Boston Whaler, adding a cabin. With such a craft, I thought it would be possible to get to places where roads didn't go.

I didn't carry through with that sketch, but it fell into the hands of Jim Saddler, who already owned a whaler, and his boat carpenter friend, Bruce Good, built a cabin as it looked in the drawing. Jim was a west-coast surfer, and because of his understanding of big waves, he often used that whaler to ride ocean crests off the outer coast of Vancouver Island.

Only days after that Muchalat Inlet experience, I received word from Don Robertson that a stout fifty-four-foot-long vessel, *Nipentuck*, was being offered as a loan to the Shantymen. A doctor in Victoria owned it. Don knew the man and seemed favourable to his generosity, but left acceptance of his offer up to me.

A great idea, I thought, *but what can I do with a boat that size alone?*

It so happened at that time that Phil Henry dropped in to see Rachel and me. Phil and I had served nearly two years together on the tug *Carol Foss* in Puget Sound. Like me, he was familiar with navigable waters between Washington and Alaska but had limited familiarity with off-the-beaten places up through British Columbia.

We looked at *Nipentuck* together and concluded it to be solid and safe. I purchased several marine charts and began mapping out a three-week voyage to places beyond road systems inside northern Vancouver Island. The voyage was to be a sampling of needs in an area earlier well served by the Columbia Coast Mission.

Our plan was to anchor, drift, or tie *Nipentuck* in selected spots, to act as a mother ship. Phil would remain with the vessel. I would then use the vessel's aluminum outboard-powered skiff to move around and meet people. Richard Parker, a promising young Nanaimo man, asked to join the voyage.

We ran the few-days distance from Victoria to Port Harvey (off Johnstone Strait), anchored for the night, and the next morning, I used the aluminum skiff to visit two families in cabins nearby, and then set off in the direction of Chatham Channel.

Phil and Richard remained with the ship.

Moving through the frigid air, I sensed I was becoming hypothermic, so I dug out a scrap of sheet plastic from the bottom of the boat and wrapped it around my trunk as a windbreak.

Assuming that would be enough to keep me warm, I continued through the Blow Hole on to Bones Bay and to the big cannery building. With more difficulty than I had imagined, I got out, stood, and then walked stiffly to the house, where I was readily welcomed in by wholesome and handsome Bill Berry and his lovely, gracious wife, Marilyn.

Seeing my chilled condition, Bill seated me close to the oil stove, and Marilyn brought coffee and something to eat. This was the beginning of a friendship that continues to this day.

The morning chill had lifted by the time I was ready to return, but even so, I was extremely cold when I got back to *Nipentuck*. Radiant heat from the galley range and a hot drink was the cure.

We anchored and drifted in numerous places over the following days. I used the aluminum boat with its outboard to visit various places and people.

I was talking with a lady at a float house off Wells Passage when a cat brushed affectionately past my legs. "What's your cat's name?" I asked.

"Money," she replied.

"Money?"

"Yes," she said. "It was my mother's sense of humour; she gave us Money as a wedding gift. Later," she continued, "Money had kittens, so we took them to her and said, 'Here's your change!'"

Nipentuck drifted off Shawl Bay. I went in with the skiff and secured to a float close to a crew of men making up a boom of logs. One man, Alf, who was obviously in charge, introduced himself. My arrival aroused the curiosity of children in the nearby float house (Alf's family). Their faces were pressed against the window glass.

I explained that I was a missionary, and that I had no intention of interrupting his work. "But," I said, "with your permission, I'd like to visit your family." Alf looked at me with his head cocked most skeptically, so I continued. "I brought colouring books and crayons for the children."

His eyes narrowed as he continued to study me, then he said, "Yes, that would be fine."

The children—Stanley, around age thirteen, and sisters ranging down in age—were pleased to have a visitor. All immediately began talking and happily colouring. Their mother said nothing. Alf came in, looked around, seemed satisfied, and left.

It happened three times.

After perhaps an hour, I said goodbye at the house and was just readying to leave in the skiff when Alf turned from his men, came over, and after several questions and with deep sincerity, asked me to come again.

It was nine years later when I met Alf with Stanley again. Stanley remembered my earlier visit clearly, what I had worn, what we had talked about, and how we had coloured pictures together.

Little did I realize the bond that would develop between Alf and me in the following decades, especially after he retired out of logging and moved to Hyde Creek near Port McNeill. I was by his side in 2004, when he lay dying in a hospital bed in Victoria. Days later, I conducted his funeral at Port McNeil.

That 1972 voyage included many places and people. There was a little indentation in the shoreline at one place where there was a small floating cabin. I called out several times when approaching. No answer. I tied the skiff, climbed out, knocked loudly, and called again. No answer. I stepped inside the unlocked door and called.

No one was there.

I prepared to leave a note, when to my surprise, I found one on the table. It was signed by Dan Somebody. The words went something like this, with no punctuation: "Who reads this note I gone to Blind Channel to find a doctor do not know if I will be back please leave food for Mike that is the cat"

I set out food for Mike, although I never did see him, and left a note for Dan. I learned later that Dan had returned to the cabin but only for a short time before he died.

I've often wondered what happened to Mike.

ʿYearround Happenings

PHIL AND I returned *Nipentuck* to its place in Victoria after the last chapter's voyage, and I continued as an itinerant missionary, again using my truck and camper.

I was home nearing Christmas when the phone rang. I picked it up and talked to the mellow, self-assured voice of Gloria Troll, the matron at a girl's school in Victoria.

The last thing her mother had told her when she took the job was NOT to bring anybody home at Christmastime.

Her mother knew her well. Gloria had taken two girls under her wing, one from Hong Kong and the other from Kuala Lumpur. They had no place to go over the winter break.

She had already gotten permission from Superintendent Don Robertson to take the girls to Camp Ross at Pachena Bay. What she wanted from me was to lead the way to the place, which was a legitimate request.

The camp was just over one hundred miles of driving from Nanaimo, and about forty of those were on logging roads. There truly was a danger of getting lost; well-traveled sections serving active logging areas could easily be mistaken for the main route.

I continued thinking about the woman's voice after hanging up the receiver. Although we had never met, I had the strangest feeling that I already knew her.

Days later, Gloria—a hardy woman with a "GO TEAM! GO!" face and dimples—arrived at our house with two delicately framed girls. Shortly thereafter, we were off for the west coast, with Gloria's tangerine-coloured Volkswagen Beetle closely following my Courier.

We arrived at the camp without incident.

The roar of breakers could be heard through a windbreak of trees. A walk across the three-acre front yard led to a path through a lightly forested area that opened to an expansive sandy beach. This was beautiful Pachena Bay—a primitive place in the experience of her schoolgirl guests. Gloria had to show them how to use an outhouse.

Ron and Joan McKee were the off-season camp caretakers. Gloria had heard of Joan, and vice versa, but they had never met and both had imagined the other to be old. As it turned out, Gloria was twenty-six and Joan was twenty-seven. That day was the start of a friendship that continued for more than four decades. Then on April 10, 2013, after a three-month bout with cancer, Gloria moved on to the mansion prepared for her. (gloriatroll@heaven.calm)

Gloria and the girl's Christmastime outing may have changed the course of Camp Ross, which in time became better known as Pachena. Up until then, it had always been a summer camp. Ron McKee suggested activating the place for functions during off-season months. I shared the idea with Don Robertson and he agreed, so we began preparing for a ten-day men's retreat to happen in February.

Some that assembled on the appointed day were men I had been visiting as a missionary, and others were ones Don Robertson knew. Somebody brought a young lady from somewhere. I never knew how she happened to be included, but her presence was a delightful addition to the gathering and a help to Joan in the kitchen. This was Mona, who described herself as a descendent of somebody named Banfield (note the "n") for whom the nearby fishing village of Bamfield was named, but misspelled.

The retreat proved to be a good thing. For some, Pachena was the space needed to separate from old haunts and bad habits—a place that provided nourishing meals, laughter around the table, and the non-judgmental manner of Ron and Joan McKee. I was the sole Bible teacher, and my style was to use a chalkboard to illustrate as I moved along through the Book of John. Mine was an application type of teaching that encouraged people not to struggle with things not understood but to act on things that were.

Those that attended wanted others to have the opportunity to experience such a retreat; we proposed another ten-day retreat for the next month, and it too proved to be a very good thing. In that case, sessions were not only for men. Joan McKee, who was a gifted teacher, conducted many of the sessions.

Ron went about a wide range of camp chores, while keeping the wood-famished furnace going. He was never too busy for one needing to talk. By genuine interest, kind understanding, and constructive words, he was often able to unlock the prison of a troubled person's mind.

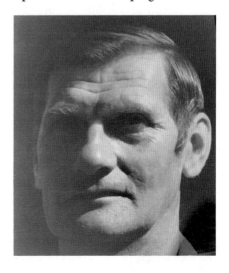

George Loewen, or Uncle George as we called him, joined the Pachena effort in 1975. He had been a church pastor and then a Shantymen missionary in northern British Columbia. In his years of ministry, he had married thirty-seven couples, yet somehow managed to escape marriage himself. His Bible knowledge and experience with people were valued assets. It eventually was Joan, Uncle George, and I, each having our own distinctive style, who formed a threesome of teachers over the next years.

People attending sessions often encouraged others. Jerry Bickerton, for example, who had attended the first retreat, sent his brother-in-law Mike Gibson. Mike, in his forties, returned home a changed man—so different that his mother, Sheila (an elegant woman and the prim and proper widowed wife of a former British officer in India) came next, and when she did, there was a typical assortment of personalities there.

One was Clyde Kelly. Clyde had hair everywhere, with only eyes for a face. The most unlikely Sheila and Clyde became instant buddies. One day, I walked into the classroom as Clyde was combing his beard forward just inches from Sheila's face, while saying, "Baa, baa, baa!" like a sheep. She was giggling happily, like a little girl.

Joan McKee gained the nickname Petunia during that time. It all started when she was singing the children's song, "I'm a Lonely Little Petunia in an Onion Patch" while sitting between Ron and me after we had eaten raw onions.

The Petunia name was indelibly attached when Jim McAlonan and Rod Mattingsly adapted the words from the song, "Country Road," ending with the chorus, *Logging roads, take me home, where I belong, West Pachena, Petunia Mama, logging roads, take me home.* They sang it several times over the following days—enough to thoroughly reinforce the name. Over time the "Mama" part was dropped, and to this day, she is widely known as Petunia.

There was something about Petunia that made her "Mama" to most everyone at the camp. Perhaps it was due to her pioneering background—she had grown up on a farm outside Duncan on Vancouver Island, without running water or electricity. Or maybe it was her always caring about people … or maybe because she had taught Grades 1 through 5 for several years. For whatever reason, Petunia, a wiry woman just over five-feet tall, had an amazing way of making things happen while also making things special for everyone.

She and Ron were a powerful team. Ron was the son of Reverend William Ormistan McKee, who was somewhat of a legend in his day. Known for his readiness in the pulpit, or beside a hospital bed, or at a graveside, his help as a minister was as close as his phone or a knock on the door. Ron, like his father, was kind, generous, ready, helpful, and understanding, but unlike his father, he was satisfied with encouraging people always out of sight of recognition. His gift was simply being sure things were running well.

All these Pachena things were happening at a time when the West Coast Lifesaving Trail had become a popular destination for hikers from many parts of the world. The north end of the trail started from one corner of the Pachena property and continued south along a most perilous stretch of coast, referred to as the Graveyard of the Pacific. The trail carried on for forty-seven arduous miles and ended at Port Renfrew.

Stories were told of people who survived shipwrecks then perished in the hostile forest jungle on shore. In 1907, the trail was pushed through for the sole purpose of preventing that happening. Telephone wires were strung the full length. Shelters with phones were spaced at intervals along the way. Linemen regularly patrolled, moving from cabin to cabin (placed at intervals along the great stretch). The need as a life-saving trail slowly disappeared, due to more reliable means of navigation and the greater reliability of ships.

Pachena's front yard, as said, was the hiker's rallying point for starting the trail from the north end. Pachena's big kitchen was very often the welcoming place for wet, cold, and hungry people ending the trail after days of punishing hiking from the south end.

You can see how, with the trail, the programs, sessions, and many other exposures, Pachena became widely known. There was never a charge to anyone, yet somehow, costs were always met.

God So Provideth

INVOLVEMENT AT PACHENA carried a good reward for anyone who went there, whether for a program or to help out. Some took part for a time and later moved into some kind of Christian service at home or abroad. Meanwhile, there was a nucleus of people who served the work diligently and sacrificially. One lady referred to these as "camp tramps."

As I saw it, the way to deal with that kind of talk was to invent a program, which we did, calling it "Field Training." Those truly involved were thereafter called "trainees." Over time, various classes and different practical exercises were developed that taught such things as first aid, food handling, vehicle maintenance, navigation, boat handling, and seamanship.

By the mid-1970s, as programs and other things were going on, Pachena provided staff and workers to summer happenings at Camp Henderson at Rupert Arm on northern Vancouver Island. Petunia detailed and coordinated things at both camps.

Ron built an information booth early on, with the intent of giving helpful information to those about to begin hiking the West Coast Trail. The booth, often using trainees to staff it, also welcomed weary folks just finishing the hike. Many had blisters or burns or other minor medical concerns.

When Parks Canada heard about his efforts, they provided pieces to build a substantial A-frame building.

The A-shapes were assembled on the ground and raised into their vertical position by a rope attached to my Ford Courier.

One day a group of four or five guys, having just completed the West Coast Trail, were invited into the lodge's big kitchen. One fellow lingered after the others left. He seemed pained. When outside of hearing, he asked Petunia, "Do you have anything for diaper rash?" The poor fellow had worn his skin raw hiking the trail in wet blue jeans.

In the history of happenings, word came from a Mr. Jans Jundo (or something like that), who was chief honcho for MacMillan Bloedel's thriving logging operation at Franklin River. He wanted to meet me.

I drove to the logging office, stepped up to an expansive front desk, and told the girl behind the counter my name and that Mr. Jundo had asked for me. She turned, walked down the long hallway, and spoke to someone through an open door before returning. A man stepped out into the hall and beckoned me to join him in his office.

He said that he had two wooden buildings that had become surplus, and wondered if they or their materials might be of use to Pachena's operation.

I said that they would, and in the days following, a team was dispatched to disassemble the structures and transport the pieces to Pachena. Ron and others immediately set about building a clinic for serving the minor medical needs of campers and hikers.

Pachena's shop had become a catch-it-all, mostly for junk. When emptying and cleaning the place, I found four different gallons of oil-based wood stains. One was leather brown, another was cherry red, and two were different browns, which I stirred together and used. When finished, it looked as if the clinic and the lodge were stained from the same batch. White trim completed the job. It was dedicated into service in early September 1974.

Hikers often arrived on the grounds in a state of near exhaustion. Some had minor injuries and were treated at the clinic. All craved carbohydrates and were given oranges, chocolate-chip cookies, or heavily frosted pieces of cake.

The Pachena lodge and clinic had its own well and water system, but there was no convenient place for hikers to get water except from the lodge. The earth was tapped and water was found near the A-frame—fresh, cool, crystal clear water filtered to perfection by the sandy soil in that location, especially refreshing after the tainted brownish water hikers had been drinking from the streams flowing out from heavily forested areas.

Hiking wasn't always fun. One lone hiker laboured under the weight of a heavy pack through days of rain. His feet slogged on as he came to a clearing. Continuing on and looking down with absent eyes, he suddenly came upon a helicopter with a Parks Canada work crew sitting inside. They were about to start up and lift off. Somebody opened a door and asked, "Do you want a ride?"

He climbed in, sat down, and even before he had removed his dripping pack, the craft was in the air. Minutes later, the helicopter landed in the big front yard at Pachena, and the work crew hurried through pelting rain and into the lodge's warm and welcoming kitchen. The bewildered hiker wandered aimlessly about for a time then plodded toward the building. I opened the door and helped remove his sodden pack.

He sat with his hands clasped around a cup of hot chocolate fully detached from the enthusiastic conversations around him. Noting his disconnection, I asked, "What are you going to do when you realize this is just a dream?"

After some hesitation, he said, "I was just thinking about that."

In addition to West Coast Trail hikers, field-training programs, and other things, Pachena often hosted field trips for high school and college groups. Petunia worked together with leaders to coordinate activities. Those in training served as staff. Gloria Troll, daughter of Joe Troll, owner of Troll's fabulous and famous seafood restaurant, always took the lead in the kitchen.

The leader of one college group said that he wanted salmon served for one main meal during their stay. Gloria said that she had none but would pray about it. A short time later, Billy Happynook happened by with a nice salmon. Learning of this, the fellow questioned Gloria's faith, since there was only one fish and thirty-five or more in the group.

The next morning, the fish plant in nearby Bamfield phoned, saying that they had some fish they wanted to give: salmon that were a bit small for processing. Gloria and Dan Sheffield drove to the place and were given two big totes totaling around five hundred pounds of fish in all. When the leader saw it, he told Gloria, "I think you can stop praying now."

Overturned Dory

I DESIGNED AND built my first surf dory at home in Nanaimo in 1974. Chet McArthur, a young man with sort of a bulldog personality, helped build a second one in the shop at Pachena.

Each dory used six rowers and one to steer, and could be carried from the lodge to the sea by its crew. With the added weight of oars and sea anchor and line, carrying it was made easier by using a cart—a two-wheeled contrivance fashioned from the rear axle and wheels of something found in the brush near the camp. A wooden pole was added as a tongue for steering.

Carting a dory on two wheels worked so well that its crew would actually run it to the beach, and because of such speed, somebody named the cart "Jehu," the name of a guy on a chariot written about in 2 Kings 9:20, where it was said, "He driveth furiously."

By summer 1975, Pachena was offering rowing camps, using Nelson Duncan's hand-built cedar castle on Copper Island in Barkley Sound as a destination base.

The dories were kept at Pachena through the winter months, and were quite often taken out for fun and adventure by those in training. Pachena Bay, facing the open Pacific, was a good place for teaching seamanship. Depending on conditions, getting off a surf beach could be difficult, and getting back safely to shore even more so.

One November day, the surf was up, and it was a good day to practice beach landings using the sea anchor. We shoved off the beach and out into the deep.

Next, was getting back.

The normal procedure was this: When preparing to land on a beach, the bow of the dory is brought around to face the waves then backed toward the beach stern first. While moving backwards under strict control of oars, a sea anchor is deployed from the bow, followed by a length of line that is made fast. Upon landing, and by command of the steersman, two rowers hop out and steady the dory as all the rest quickly disembark and carry the dory above the reach of the next wave.

Some of the guys begged to surf the dory to the beach. I eventually yielded; if nothing else, doing it wrong would demonstrate that a boat cannot be brought in safely that way.

I was on the steering oar, and my back was to the breakers. The bow of the dory faced the beach, ready to surf in. I was able to control things when the first sizable breaker slammed into the transom. It happened again, and I was again able to prevent broaching by quick action with the steering oar, but the third wave hit with such force that it knocked me out of the seat and into the bottom of the boat, which was by then half full of water. I didn't lose the steering oar, but because of being on my back and lying in the bottom, the dory turned sideways to the sea and burst uncontrollably ahead on the next curling crest. Everyone spilled out, and the dory turned over. Being in shallows, some were able to scamper to safety on the sand.

The upside-down dory was drawn back by the next great wave into some depth.

Someone shouted that Petunia was under it! One of the guys pushed his way through the swirling water and grabbed her by the only visible part: her hand, waving out from underneath.

The dory was wrestled ashore, and the water was dumped out.

Weather had by then turned rainy and cold and most were chilled and shivering. Realizing the incident could leave lasting scars if not brought to a good end, I insisted that the dory be taken out into the deep and brought in properly, using the sea anchor and with the control of oars.

We did; it worked perfectly, and all seemed pleased by their skill. It was the last time I heard talk about surfing a dory in.

It was on that same stretch of beach that we baptized Jimmy McAlonan, an animated young man with body movements that resembled the old ragtime music of the 1920s. It was a nice day and a solemn occasion when a small group gathered on the sand above the reach of waves. Uncle George, Jimmy, and I waded out into the sea and took up position for the ceremony, facing those on shore.

I was on Jimmy's right and Uncle George was on his left—three in a line, arms locked across shoulders in the good spirit of the occasion.

Being an ordained minister and fully qualified to conduct such a service, Uncle George did the talking. Who knows how many different people he had baptized?

He spoke a long time. Meanwhile, I noted a large ocean swell over my shoulder. It was taking shape some distance behind our backs. Uncle George droned on. Bless him. Meanwhile, I watched as the big wave drew nearer. Uncle George finally got to the punch line, if for a moment you can imagine a baptismal service having such a thing. He said, "I now baptize thee, James McAlonan, in the name of the Father, and the Son, and the Ho—"

The huge wave swept over all three of us. We found ourselves on our hands and knees in the sand as the water receded. I can only guess that the Holy Spirit decided to speak for Himself.

Long Trial Run

MANY OF THOSE in training had sufficient skills to engage in missionary projects, so we introduced a second level of training in 1975 and called it the "Student Missionary Program."

That led to a number of things, including sending out land teams to places

as far as Washington State, and sea teams, using Brian Burkholder's fifty-some-foot-long fishboat *Kolberg* for missionary voyages to places as distant as Wrangell, Alaska, the Queen Charlotte Islands, and on the British Columbia coast. Folks at one place showed in their guest book that the last missionaries had visited thirty-one years earlier.

Debbie Forney, often called Sunshine, had been part of everything since 1973 and was stationed in Victoria, where she visited the elderly in private homes, nursing homes, and hospitals. She was later assigned to work with Gloria Troll at Sandspit in the Queen Charlotte Islands (Haida Guaii).

The two pitched in, helping local storekeepers, Gordon and Gloria Schiller, at the local grocery. This gave them the opportunity to meet and get to know most everyone in town.

On Sunday mornings, they'd clean up the community hall and have Sunday school for children. Over time, that effort grew to include mothers and eventually whole families. Something like "church" came out of their work and was handed over to the Canadian Sunday School Mission. Gloria and Debbie were credited as being, would you believe, the church fathers.

At one point, I went to visit them. It was a damp, cold, miserable day. The first leg of the trip was by floatplane from Nanaimo to Vancouver. Being familiar with up-coast weather in the off-season, I found it difficult to convince myself that I really wanted to go there.

I placed luggage on the scale in resigned anticipation of receiving the boarding pass, not realizing that there were two different airlines—Coastal Pacific and Pacific Coastal. It came as a surprise when the man behind the counter, polite but with a starchy face and phony accent, said, "I'm sorry, sir, but we fly only to the Hawaiian Islands."

The image of gentle palms and warm sunshine came to mind, so I said, "Sounds good to me."

Not amused, he pointed across the terminal to the desk where I was *supposed* to be.

It was also in 1975 that I worked with people in training to build a modified motor dory, called *CV-1* (short for *Coastal Vessel One*). It had to be seaworthy, beachable, and able to travel long distances fast.

One reason for building it was to teach boat-building skills, and another was because (when finished and tested) I wanted to give it to Shantyman missionary Joe Ottom, who lived with his family at Sointula on Malcolm Island. He had his truck and could go by public ferry to Alert Bay on Cormorant Island or Port McNeill, which connected to Vancouver Island's road systems, but he lacked the means to visit people living in many coastal areas that surrounded to the north and east of him.

Since waters around his location could be very rough, the boat had to be strong and able. I knew there would be those who would question the safety and seaworthiness of such a small craft.

CV-1 was powered by a three-cylinder Johnson 70 set in a well two feet forward of the stern. An upside-down "U" in the transom made it possible to tilt the motor up. That configuration made it easily possible, if needed, to change a propeller.

After the boat was completed, it was launched at nearby Bamfield, run to Port Alberni, then placed on a trailer and transported across the Island to French Creek near Parksville. There, I made ready for a trial run to Alaska and back.

By then, August had turned to September.

My thoughtful and highly competent friend Ken Menzies joined me for the run. The weather was warm and wind was calm as CV-1 headed out the breakwater and into the Strait of Georgia. Our first stop was at Sisters Island Lightstation, an isolated government-built structure reminiscent of Alcatraz.

Ken nosed the boat up close to the shore, and I jumped off and climbed up the rocks. Ken stayed with the boat and drifted, while I went inside the building, found the keeper, and had a delightful hour of visiting together. Back again with Ken, we continued around the upper end of Texada Island and went into the harbour at Powell River, where our arrival aroused some curiosity. We stood on the float answering questions before moving to the fuel float.

Coastal road systems end not far north of Powell River, so the people that live beyond are reliant on their boats to get around, and on freight boats and oil barges to deliver freight and fuel. Floatplanes also play a huge role, carrying people, mail, and parcels, and parts. Pilots are venerated. High-speed water taxis seen today came after 1975.

CV-1 continued at a good turn of speed, with wavelets pattering on the bottom of the hull sounding like ping-pong balls. Over the next days, Ken and I likened the sounds of the different waveforms to baseballs, basketballs, pillows, marshmallows, and mattresses.

We tied up for the night at the public float on Stuart Island.

The next morning, the third of September, the motor was started, lines were let go, and we were off, but out in the channel, the motor suddenly quit. I *thought* I had rotated the valve from one gas tank to the other but had actually turned both tanks off! Once we figured it out, we were late for slack water in Gillard Passage and Dent Rapids but continued anyway through eddies and swirls.

We then came to the place shown on navigation charts as *Devil's Hole*. A massive slow-turning vortex had formed already, and before fully realizing the horrible potential, *CV-1* was down in the swirl not far from the hole. Luckily, just as quickly, *CV-1* was back up the other side and out.

We tied at Shoal Bay in mid-morning. Two men, from two boats, came out on the float to greet us. One called himself "the Eskimo." He reminded us of a friendly pirate. The other, George Weeks, was a fisheries patrol officer, and expressed concern for a man, Rodney, who had settled in the mouth of Forward Harbour. He said that Rodney had been too long away from society. After goodbyes, Ken and I carried on through passages and went into Forward Harbour.

Rodney's shack was perched high and dry on float logs. *CV-1* nosed into the shallows and was beached. A cat and kittens came out to greet us. We pushed off into deeper water and tied to an anchored raft. After lunch, we lay on the raft and enjoyed the warm sun. Reflections of sunlight off the rippled sea made thin ribbon shapes on the orange hull of *CV-1*.

The stillness was broken by footsteps on gravel, so we quickly climbed onboard *CV-1* and motored to the shore. It was Rodney and Norman returning from Norman's place some distance away by trail through the forest.

The 1960s and 1970s were a time in North America when many young people ventured outside the norms of establishment. It was hard to know why. In some cases, it was in reaction to America's military involvement in Vietnam. In others, it was a mere expression of rights and freedoms made possible by more money, easy travel, and less personal accountability.

Rodney was intrigued with *CV-1*. He sat in the operator's seat with his hands on the steering wheel, making motor sounds with his mouth. He begged Norman to come inside. Norman quietly objected, "I hate neat boats."

ℋavelock Fyfe

A STIFF WESTERLY wind was blowing the next morning as *CV-1* entered Johnstone Strait, making it too rough to continue; the strait is known for its steep seas, especially when the current opposes the wind direction.

We found shelter in a little spot around and behind Tuna Point, and tied to a string of logs leading to a house on the shore. Originally a float house, it was now perched high up the beach at a decided slant.

As we started toward the house, walking on the floating logs, a man in his sixties stepped out and welcomed us.

This was Havelock Fyfe.

He placed a handmade cigarette in his mouth, lit it, and used his left thumb to rid a fleck of tobacco from his lip. Over the next hours, it became evident that his fidgeting with a fleck was a nervous habit. Otherwise, he seemed quite normal.

Havelock wanted us to join him for supper, so I went to the boat and brought back a jar of sauerkraut. Conversation continued over boiled potatoes, sauerkraut, mild onion slices, and codfish. When ready to leave, Havelock insisted on giving us several onions to take with us.

Ken and I walked the logs back to the boat in darkness.

The wind and chop were down the next morning. We continued to Alert Bay, then Port McNeill, and then Sointula, where the boat was beached on the gravel as the tide was receding, in order to change oil in the lower leg of the outboard.

The slant of the beach was just right for the vee of the bottom of the craft, making it level enough to make and serve coffee to the people drawn by curiosity to the orange-hulled *CV-1* on their beach. Interest was stimulated even more when learning ours was a trial run to Alaska and back.

After floating free, *CV-1* was secured in the harbour, and we walked to the Joe Ottom home. There we enjoyed supper, and visiting, and baths.

We traveled onward the next morning and into Allison Harbour when fog began to obscure navigational landmarks. There, we came upon a boat at anchor. A man came out on its deck and motioned us alongside.

Garth Esmond was a lean and extremely fit abalone diver who often spent eight or more hours in the water each day. Visiting continued over lunch; then noting that fog was lifting, we were off.

The sea and sky became blue, and waves were topped with dazzling white as we continued past Cape Caution and into the full influence of wind and waves from the northwest. Over and over, the bow of *CV-1* rose and dropped abruptly into the trough that followed.

Nearing the southern end of Calvert Island, the waves took on a rounded shape, allowing the throttle to be brought up a few notches. Before long, the craft was up to regular speed, racing along great ridges and deep valleys of ocean swells.

Once in the lee of Calvert Island, we continued to Namu. By then, being late, *CV-1* was tied quietly amongst commercial fish boats. The next morning, we visited different ones, including the one belonging to Frank Johnson and his wife. When invited to step inside the cabin of his boat, people from a nearby vessel wanted to squeeze in too.

Before leaving, Ken and I hiked to the lake, with one of the fishermen joining us.

The next stop was Bella Bella for gas, and we were off again.

Swells were marching in from Milbanke Sound, so we took the option of negotiating Reid Passage, which begins in a rock-strewn area behind Ivory Island. We carried on to Klemtu, where *CV-1* was tied to the old cannery float.

After supper, we followed the boardwalk into the village and to the school, where in the home of the principal we had tea and met the two new teachers. This was their first week at Klemtu and first-ever introduction to village life.

CV-1 was off again the next morning. We stopped at Butedale for gas and then continued on in the direction of Prince Rupert—another hundred nautical miles. An afternoon breeze began to freshen at Morning Reef, and in time, lesser wavelets turned to more significant whitecaps. Water from the Skeena River made the sea emerald green.

Upon arrival, *CV-1* was secured in Cow Bay. Our average speed from Klemtu had been 21.3 knots, and the sense of traveling and bouncing continued while walking ashore for supper.

The next morning, after buying fresh grocery items, and after filling gas tanks, we were off, first to Port Simpson for a brief stop and then on to Ketchikan. Being too late for Customs, we remained aboard. The first half of *CV-1*'s run to Alaska and back was complete.

ℒatitudes North

KEN AND I had our morning habits. I usually woke at dawn. I would light the burner under the coffee pot then turn on the cabin heater. Warmth in the cabin and the smell and taste of fresh coffee provided a good start to the day.

I'd soon hear Ken's cheery, "Good morning."

Each morning included a hearty breakfast of bacon, eggs, toast, sliced tomatoes, and fried onions—a daily reminder of Havelock Fyfe.

This particular morning, I dressed and shaved and left the boat before breakfast with the boat's Canadian Registry. I wanted to be at the Customs office at 8:00 a.m.

Something about the smell inside the building and the worn marble in the corridors made the Ketchikan Federal Building seem official.

Clearing Customs took minutes.

We left Thomas Basin after breakfast and moved to Bar Harbor in search of Richard and Doris Lowe. They had sold their old *Gypsy Jean* and were now living in Ketchikan on their new sailboat, a boat I had never seen and didn't know the name of. Ken suggested we ask another sailboat owner, since (he reasoned) one sailboat owner usually knows another.

CV-1 motored up close to a trimaran where Jeff Edwards was working. When asked, he said, "Richard and Doris live on the blue sailboat, *Firewater,* on this same float."

At that moment, Doris happened along and was delighted to see me and meet Ken. After a brief visit on the float, I explained that Ken and I would be off for the next hours then return so we could visit with Richard.

We traveled to the upper end of Gravina Island and motored up to a float house complete with floating greenhouse garden. A woman, introducing herself as Gina, welcomed us. The cabin was cheerfully decorated with pictures and handcrafts. In one corner was a piano, and on the post inside the door was a leather belt stuffed with bullets and a big .44.

We returned to supper with Richard and Doris on their ketch, *Firewater*. Doris had prepared salmon steaks, and our happy talk continued late into the evening.

CV-1 left for Prince Rupert the next morning. At twenty-plus knots, the eighty-five nautical miles were travelled pretty fast. After clearing Canadian Customs, we returned to the boat. A young man from Malay came by to talk through the open window then took us for a driving tour, first to Port Edward and on to a vantage overlooking Prince Rupert.

We continued southward the next day. Weather was good at the start, but a forceful southeast wind gave us the idea to divert into Hartley Bay. When the wind eased, we carried on to Butedale.

Once there, we hurriedly climbed the mountain to the lake and scrambled back down before sundown. I stopped to watch the hydro generators that had continued to turn out undeviating electricity, by then for thirty-three years.

We spoke with Ralph and Isabel Maloney on a boat contracted to Fisheries patrol in that area. Ralph told us of a barge that had struck Hewitt reef in Hiekish Narrows. A gash along the side of its bottom had allowed the sea to flood in. It slowly lay over and capsized, and its deck-load of mobile homes, construction equipment, and containers had spilled into the sea. Salvage operations were taking place in nearby Khutz Inlet.

Ken and I were off the next morning to see. We landed *CV-1* between two gigantic skegs on the overturned barge. A man I assumed to be a sailor on the nearby salvage tug, *Sudbury II*, caught our line to tie there. Someone told me a few minutes later that he was the vessel's captain.

A second barge with cranes had been brought in to assist the salvage. After a time being shown around the operation, Ken and I were off to Bella

Bella and to the gas float. Dozens of people were on the pier, some sitting, some standing, but all watching as I, the center of attention, held the nozzle.

A few hours later, *CV-1* arrived at Namu, where Ken and I were warmly greeted by people on commercial boats we'd met on our way north. They asked what had gone wrong and why we were back so soon. I assured them that nothing had gone wrong and that we were just now returning from Alaska. I could see that such a distance in so little time was beyond seven-and-eight-knot thinking.

We continued southward. It was foggy in Queen Charlotte Sound, so I set a course that should put us a mile west off Egg Island, and when at that point, I stopped the engine, drifted, and listened for the fog whistle from the light-station. When confirmed, *CV-1* was again off in blinding fog. Huge ground swells made it difficult to maintain a course with certainty.

The same action was taken off Pine Island, and when satisfied, course was set for Scarlett Point. Fog cleared and swells abated when rounding into Christie Pass. There, *CV-1* tied to a small float in a snug little spot out of all influence of the Pacific.

The next morning was a Sunday, and we were again on our way and passed a seine boat plowing its way south, obviously traveling twenty-four hours a day. Ken and I recognized passing it some days before, and those on deck recognized us too and waved enthusiastically.

CV-1 arrived at Sointula and tied in the harbour and there we had breakfast. Ken washed dishes while I shaved, and we set off on foot to the community church.

Singing could be heard as we went in and sat in the back, hoping not to disturb anyone. Joe and Helen Ottom noticed and so did the pastor, Len Perry. Having heard of the *CV-1* venture, he asked us to tell them about the trip.

The remainder of the day was spent with the Ottom family, and in the evening, others joined in visiting, including the Len Perry family.

Off again the following morning; we stopped to visit Havelock Fyfe, who was still spitting imaginary pieces of tobacco. We were then on our way for the long run that ended in darkness at Powell River.

This was a special evening for Ken. His wife, Debbie, was visiting her parents. Ken and I walked to the house together. When he knocked, Debbie opened the door, and it was just like the movies…

I returned to *CV-1* alone.

I left the harbour in the late morning and traveled around the top end of Texada Island before setting course directly for French Creek. A haze restricted visibility to perhaps a mile. I stopped the engine and drifted to prepare lunch. After washing dishes, the engine was started, and I was off.

Hints of land began to appear through the mist, and in time, the breakwater at French Creek came into view. Sport-fishing boats bobbed about near the entrance.

CV-1's trial run was complete.

After securing to a float and tidying things, I grabbed my bag and walked the small distance to the highway. Minutes later, I was the hitchhiking passenger in the front of a pickup truck that delivered me to the bus depot in Nanaimo.

I phoned Rachel, and she arrived in minutes. I opened the passenger door, got in, and sat down. She smiled sweetly and said, "You look weathered."

This finishes the chapter, except (as you remember) the boat was built for Joe Ottom's missionary work out of Sointula. A few weeks later, Joe and I were delivered to *CV-1* at French Creek. By then, we were into the foul-weather month of October.

It was blowing southeast outside the breakwater, and rough as we progressed in the direction of Denman and Hornby Islands—so rough, in fact, that I wondered if we should have stayed at French Creek. I looked across at Joe, a man of faith, full of trust and the picture of tranquility. It was hardly the Joe I knew. He was usually an excitable fellow, a cross between a bulldozer and a chainsaw.

Joe then said, "It's pretty rough out here."

"Yes," I agreed.

He then said, "It's a comfort to know the designer and builder of the boat is here."

I thought he'd been trusting the Lord!

The Lion's Den

DON ROBERTSON, LEADING missionary of the Vancouver Island branch, had retired from Canada Post at an earlier time but was now wanting to retire again—or at least step back from the responsibility of superintending Shantymen work on Vancouver Island. The head office in Toronto asked me to take his place.

Most of the administrative work could be handled from my home. I usually waited on diving into things until Rachel left for teaching and after Paul and Jim were off to school. The cats remained at home, except on the one occasion that Jim took Buster to school for Show and Tell.

Buster always liked children. Years earlier, when we lived on *Ivanhoe*, a little boy came and asked if Buster could come out and play. The boy and his friends were catching tiny fish off the edge of the float. I brought Buster out to join them and then began talking with a man standing nearby. Our visit was interrupted when the boy came up to us, tears running down both cheeks.

"What's wrong?" I asked.

"Your cat took my fish," the little fellow said.

"Where did he take it?" I questioned.

"Down there." The boy pointed at the entry leading down inside *Ivanhoe*.

"Let's have a look," I said, and took the boy where he could see Buster eating the fish most carefully around the hook.

"He likes it," the boy said, with eyes suddenly turning from distress to delight. He then happily said, "I'll catch him another one."

Buster, having a notably relaxed mental attitude, was content simply being a cat as I worked in my home office. Our elegant Russian Blue, Dusty, was much more active, often chattering at birds through the window, chasing flies, or playing little made-up cat games.

One day, she came into my office in desperate need of affection. I scooted

back from the electric typewriter and picked her up. She stood on my lap with her front paws hugging around my neck while bunting my chin. I stood up. She hung on and continued bunting. One of her hind paws was on my tummy. Seeking a place for her other back paw, she stepped on the electric typewriter's keyboard. It burst to life, and she exploded straight up, leaving me bleeding from the back of my neck and through my shirt from my belly.

In 1975, an overall director, Arthur Dixon, an elegant man and an excellent Bible teacher was appointed to head all Shantymen efforts across Canada. His office was in Toronto, Ontario.

Branches of the Shantymen existed in about a dozen places across Canada; each had their own ways of doing things. In an effort to unify, yearly conferences were held in Toronto.

My memory goes back to my first conference; it was also my first time in Toronto. Before I tell about it, and to set the stage, I need to go back even further, to those years working on the tug *Inverness*, towing logs in remote southeastern Alaska. Work on tugs paid well and could be interesting, but it was also a life of great sacrifice. A man leaves everything nice. His clothes become filthy and stiff. The smell of sulfur diesel exudes from his pores. Lift an arm, whew, and the smell burns the eyes.

A bucket of water was warmed on the galley range and taken out on the stern to take a bath—a simple matter of stripping down and washing all over. There was seldom concern for privacy, since most every place the tug went was well draped by the great curtain of nature. Washing clothes amounted to about the same thing; they were hung in the engine room to dry.

Reading material consisted of a few dog-eared pocket books, a stack of old newspapers, and several issues of *TIME* magazine, which served as a thread to civilization for a man so greatly removed from current happenings. Subjects ranged through politics, economics, men and women's fashions, and the latest shows on Broadway. I analyzed every article, considered every cover, and dissected the ads.

There was a mighty contrast between my drab world and the colorful array displayed on the covers and in the pages of *TIME*. Little related to my world, but I did gain a lot of information that nobody in my circle cared about, talked about, or asked about.

I longed for the day when there was *even a reason* to take a real bath, get dressed nicely, and do something special with Rachel and our boys. The only thing preventing this was reality—and the reality was that I was completely separated from all and everything lovely and nice.

TIME magazine said a lot about New York City. I had no desire to go there but knew Macy's and Wall Street and other influences served as a guide for fashion and business in the western world.

In time, I *did* have opportunity to take a bath and dress nicely for something special. But it was not until the Toronto conference thing that I thought to buy something *truly* up to date fashion-wise.

Finding men's fashions in Nanaimo was difficult but possible. I bought the latest of everything for that period—classy tan slacks, elegantly bloused at the bottom, balloon-toed shoes, a bright floral shirt, and socks to match.

I made the flight to Toronto in regular nice clothes, was met at the airport, and given a card listing conference session times and other details, including a few assigned engagements. I was then delivered to the home of Norm and Marge Barnes, a dear older couple who would be looking after me during my stay in the city.

That was a Saturday.

Marge asked about my Sunday assignments, which I showed her. I was to be the morning speaker at Jarvis Street Baptist (I had never heard of it).

When she heard "Jarvis Street Baptist," she got a strange look on her face. When asked what I needed to know, she answered with one word, "Nothing." As she still had a most unusual expression, I pressed for an explanation, but she remained silent.

I had to be satisfied that a Baptist church is just a Baptist church.

On the Sunday morning, now dressed in my fashionable attire—after all, this was Toronto—and being delivered to the Gothic-style stone building, I began to comprehend Marge's reluctance to say anything. Jarvis Street was Canada's largest Baptist Church and part of the Toronto Baptist Seminary and Bible College.

I was seated with others on the platform and was the only one dressed in colorful modern attire. Three choirs behind me were wearing somber robes, and everybody else on the platform was wearing black.

I had made a few notes while on the airplane, in the likelihood I'd be speaking somewhere, but this was way outside anything I had imagined.

It was eventually my turn to deliver the morning message. The pulpit was adjustable. The last thing I remember before stepping behind it was a man in a dark suit, best described as a chauffeur in a motorcade, who politely asked (in 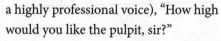 a highly professional voice), "How high would you like the pulpit, sir?"

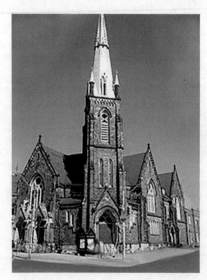

I motioned a line across my middle, and the man cranked the mechanism and stepped back. I took position behind it and prayed, *Lord, you got me into this.*

I had my few scribbled notes and likely followed them.

Would you believe that, when in Toronto the following year, Jarvis Street specifically asked for me? This time I wore an unimaginative conventional dark suit and was never asked again.

Going back to the subject of unifying the work of the Shantymen across Canada, Vancouver Island had used boats from the early thirties, and those involved had left a great and lasting legacy. Now with Vancouver Island's present team, the work, modeled by its history, was alive again.

In all of Vancouver Island's past, there had never been an appeal for money, nor had there ever been a crippling shortage. Our refusal to change that policy and refusal to send out people to raise money was offensive to the Toronto administration. It was also offensive that Vancouver Island used boats, and crews, and teams.

All came to a head in Victoria in November 1979, when the overall director came from the Toronto office and met with leaders of the Vancouver Island branch, including Petunia and Uncle George. The man spoke from a written list of demands, each followed by the phrase, "If for conscience sake you cannot agree, you will be requested to resign."

Conscience? Daniel, by certain unshakable beliefs, was thrown into the lions' den.

Unfinished Basement

AFTER THAT MEETING, Uncle George and I returned to the Miller family home where we were billeted. We went to bed without conversation.

Mine was a deeply troubled night, knowing my conscience could not continue with an administration that sought to destroy what God had led.

The next morning, Uncle George said that he had tossed and turned through the night too. When realizing that we were thinking the same thing, we became curious about Petunia's state of mind, and decided to find out. She was staying at her mother's place in Duncan.

With me, it was hurt. With Uncle George, it was sadness. With Petunia, it was anger, and I mean *anger!* I was strangely comforted knowing there were three of us.

As word of that meeting spread, it was clear that there was no change in how other branches of the Shantymen across Canada felt; many expressed how sad and disappointing it was that the Toronto administration was unable to wrap their minds around the wonder of Vancouver Island's long-enduring work.

Gloria Troll and Debbie Forney (now Debbie Maxie) were at that time stationed in the Queen Charlotte Islands. Learning what had happened, they (like others who were part of the great team) simply continued without a visible organization and without means of support.

Business and fellowship meetings had traditionally been the second Tuesday of every month, so on that day the next month, seventeen persons gathered; all knew that *some* kind of bona-fide organization was needed to continue.

John (Johnny) Duerksen, who was well informed in matters of business and administration, was automatically given the lead. He first ascertained that we were all on the same frequency. A steering committee was formed, and that included Petunia and me, who were able to pursue the matter the next day.

We drove to Victoria, parked, paid the meter, and noted the time. I stepped up to a counter, where I had previously done government business, and told the lady our purpose for coming.

"You've come to the wrong place," she said, "but if you will step outside, I will show you where you *need* to go."

From that vantage, she pointed toward a brick courtyard some distance away. "Walk to the far corner of those red bricks, and you'll find a stairway that leads to a second floor. When you get to the top, you will be at a counter. Ask for my friend Rose."

We did as directed and were met by the only evident person. "Rose?" I asked.

"Yes," she said.

I told her how I knew her name and then explained why we were there. She immediately set about gathering forms and then explained what each was for and how to fill them out.

Petunia and I returned to the vehicle. It had all taken less than half an hour. There we were in the capitol city of British Columbia, not knowing where to start or what questions to ask, and in minutes, had the forms necessary to begin the process of incorporating.

Johnny urged me to prepare a letter to people familiar with the coastal work, saying that they needed to know what was happening. I did, typically making no mention of money or needs or blame.

Some copies went out in late December 1979, and the remainder in early January 1980. The overwhelming response took me by surprise. Letters of encouragement and donations began pouring in.

An office of sorts was hurriedly set up in the unfinished basement of our home, where Anne Spencer (now Anne Burkholder) began keeping financial records and sending out commonplace receipts.

Some weeks later, a man came to me and said that he wanted to give a sizable sum of money. He knew that a mission boat would be needed. "A good one," he emphasized.

With that information, Ron McKee went to the listings and found a vessel of the right proportions for sale in Sidney. I drove to have a look and realized that it wouldn't be suitable for our use, but being in Sidney, I went to the office of the marine broker and explained what was needed. He said that his firm had nothing to offer.

I thanked him and stepped toward the door. He then stopped me, saying he had forgotten that a forty-eight-foot-long former government vessel had just been brought in. He said that he knew little about it, other than it was to be sold, and handed me a key to have a look.

I entered through the vessel's aft entry, looked around, and then went into the cold engine room. There, by the dismal lighting provided by the ship's greatly run-down bank of batteries and the flashlight in my hand, I studied the ship's various systems.

It was evident that, underneath the soil and grime, all was proper and sound. I toured the pilothouse, galley, forward and aft quarters, and their adjoining heads. Hatches and floorboards were lifted, and lastly, the condition of the peak and the lazarette were assessed.

I returned the key and thanked the broker, making no mention of what I had concluded.

I did, however, share my assessment with Ron McKee, Uncle George, and Brian Burkholder, saying that I was satisfied with what I had seen but invited them to pursue looking at other possibilities.

They did and all decided to move ahead with purchase of the *D.M.Mackay* before somebody else bought it.

When more closely considering the vessel, Brian and I discovered that its engine, a 1958 marine Rolls Royce marine diesel, was sick. Even so, after discussion, we concluded that *D.M.Mackay* would be a good purchase, even if the engine had to be replaced.

The papers were signed February 29, 1980, at the Ship's Registry in Victoria, and in the transaction the little ship became *Coastal Messenger*. Coastal Missions was still in the application stages and not yet an official entity that could own a vessel, so Brian and I became the named owners with the plan of transferring title as soon as it became possible.

We came up with a list of mechanics that had experience with Rolls Royce industrial and marine engines. One of the names, George Beddoes, was picked because he lived in Nanaimo, the same as me, but when I phoned, he sounded hesitant, saying he was retired. He agreed that he wanted to meet me.

There was a sizable piece of driftwood that resembled a sea monster beside the driveway as I drove in. Even before introducing myself, I told George that I was careful not to arouse the dragon when coming in. "Oh, that's Ernie," he said. "He would never hurt anyone."

George was very British, with the deportment of a medical specialist, and had been with Rolls Royce from 1932 to 1969, first in England and then in Canada, until he retired.

He reluctantly agreed to have a look at the engine.

Shortly after arriving on board, George, in a rather commanding voice said, "Start the engine, take the boat out, and run her up to 1800 rpm." Brian was at the controls. I stayed with George.

He went on deck and stood near the dry stack. He canted his head, while also visually studying the engine's exhaust gasses. He then reached up for a handful of exhaust, sniffed his hand, and then stepped back, cocking his ears at different angles.

I wondered if the man could be for real.

Next, we went into the engine room while the engine was still at 1800 rpm. I watched his fingers as he momentarily held each injector line. When finished and seemingly satisfied, he said with the same commanding voice, "Take her in and tie her up."

D.M.Mackay was soon secured, and when the engine was stopped, George, the Rolls Royce man, Brian, and I went into the engine room for a little conference. George explained things and I kept notes while skeptically thinking, *Nobody can diagnose an engine by mere sound, smell, and touch.*

George said, "Take the fuel pump and injectors to Fred Holmes in Vancouver; make sure Neil Herron does the work and give me a call when you get everything back."

What other choice was there but to do as he advised?

Meanwhile, with the help of many, *Coastal Messenger* was cosmetically and otherwise brought up to standard.

The engine's fuel pump was eventually returned from Vancouver, and I phoned George. This time, when he came to the vessel, he brought his rosy-cheeked wife, Gwladys (welsh variant of Gladys), explaining that he had always wanted her to see the "boat" but had never had an opportunity. That made little sense, until it was revealed that he had worked with the vessel's

design architect and had also supervised installation of that engine when the vessel was built twenty-two years earlier. In time, we learned even more. George had helped develop the marine version of that model of Rolls Royce.

Though we didn't realize it at the time, of all mechanics, no man on earth was more qualified to be of help.

Brian tended George like an operating-room nurse as injectors were installed. Meanwhile, Gwladys was with the women in the galley. We could hear eruptions of laughter from time to time through the bulkhead.

George next timed the fuel pump, set the tappets, and made other adjustments. When ready, he announced, "You may run the engine now."

The starter button was pushed. The engine rolled to a smooth start. Wow, just like that, everything was perfect. New engine. I never imaged an angel to have an English accent.

When questioned about payment, George said, "It would be payment enough if you would take Gwlad and me out where she can catch a cod."

The happy cod event soon happened, and George and Auntie Gwlad, as she was ever after called, remained our dear friends as long as they both lived.

Incorporated Society

COASTAL MISSIONS APPLICATION to become a "society" was accepted on first reading, May 7, 1980.

With society papers in hand, I went directly to the office of the Register of Shipping and asked that ownership of the vessel be transferred to the now existing Coastal Missions Society. It was promptly done, and then a sudden worried expression came over the face of John Smith, kindly gentleman and attending Registrar of Shipping. Even though there was no exchange of money in the transfer of ownership, he explained, Coastal Missions Society might have to pay tax on the "fair value" of the ship.

I asked if there was anyone I could talk to about it.

He took me to a window and pointed across to a stone building, calling attention to a particular door in its lower corner. "Go in there," he advised. "There might be *some* exception."

"What office is it?" I asked.

"Corporate and Consumer Affairs," he answered.

Carrying the sheath that included the newly approved corporate status, I stepped inside the door and a woman appeared at the counter. When the circumstance was explained, her face flushed with anger, making it clear that every last cent of tax owing would have to be paid, no matter how benevolent *anyone* thought they were.

Nothing could placate her. She abruptly turned and walked away, leaving me standing there, but as she did, she quoted something like, "The only exception is when the one giving is also a principal officer of the society."

"I qualify," I said.

"How?" she asked accusingly.

"I'm president of the board and owner of the vessel."

"Oh," she said, greatly deflated. "I'll get someone."

The irony of the situation is that I neither intended to be named as an owner of the vessel nor the president of the society. Johnny Duerksen had taken such a lead getting things started that we all assumed he would take that position. But no, the evening before the application was to be submitted, he said that he only wanted to be helpful. I allowed my name to stand but *only* to get things rolling.

The woman returned to the counter with her supervisor. After verifying certain things from documents taken from the sheath I was carrying, the man said that Coastal Missions Society was exempt from taxation. He then asked her to prepare a pink slip, whatever that meant, and keep it on file in case the matter came up again.

After the man left, she was most apologetic, saying, "It has always made me angry when I see religion misusing the system."

I told her that I felt the same way about religion, and then said, "But we are just a small group of people trying to do what the Lord is leading."

"I see that *now*," she said in soft tones. "I'm very sorry for the way I acted."

On June 1, 1980, after its commissioning in Victoria's Inner Harbour, the *Coastal Messenger* set out first to places up the British Columbia coast and into south-eastern Alaska, then the Queen Charlotte Islands and down the outside of Vancouver Island, south to Tacoma, and home before Christmas. Brian Burkholder and I alternated as skippers during that time, with crew changes at strategic places every four to six weeks.

Such voyaging, with some variation, became the pattern of yearly circuit for the following decades.

In 1986, the directors of the Coastal Missions Society approved a ten-year plan to replace the wooden *Coastal Messenger*. There was no hurry, but the wooden vessel was then twenty-seven years old, and like a car, in ten years it would be ten years older. Considering human nature, nothing would happen without a plan.

After that meeting, I began to gather information necessary to design and build a new ship. Getting exact information was quite a task before the internet. In one case, I went to the engineering department of Industrial Plastics in Vancouver.

My question seemed vague to the fellows at first. I asked, "How can I learn about plastics?" Then I explained, "I'm well-acquainted with boat building, but my experience goes back to a time before the use of plastics. Can you recommend a book, so that I can educate myself on the subject?"

One guy, apparently in charge of the office, nodded across the room to another, who then reached down to a knee-high shelf and pulled out a heavy catalogue looking publication. "Here," he said, as he pressed it into my hands. "It's yours."

Over the following weeks, I studied its pages cover to cover.

Some time after that, I happened into the shop belonging to the local tugboat outfit. My presence was no surprise. We had used their marine ways each spring to haul our vessel, but while in there this time, my eyes took note of a block of black plastic on a workbench. Curious, I walked over, rubbed it with my thumb, and felt its waxy finish.

A fellow across the shop noticed and asked, "What is it?"

Surprised that anyone had noticed me, I said "It's ultra-high, molecular-weight polyethylene ultraviolet-inhibited plastic, or UHMW UV for short."

The guy slapped his forehead and asked, "How on earth could you know that?"

"Well," I answered, "I'm that kind of guy."

Big White Bunny

TO KEEP THINGS straight, the wooden *D.M.Mackay* became *Coastal Messenger* in 1980 when we bought it. Its name was changed back to *D.M.Mackay* when sold in 1992. The name *Coastal Messenger* was legally held in reserve for the new vessel talked about next.

When the wooden vessel was sold, I dropped everything and began the design of a new steel one.

Designing a serious steel craft from scratch is much more than an artistic expression; every aspect must be verified, and in this case, I used standards set by the American Bureau of Shipping. Likewise, all systems must carefully be engineered and woven into the plan.

Design work took place in our windowless-basement furnace room, and there, day after day, I laboured alone over figures and the drawing board until January 1993, when Rachel came home talking about a "really nice" cat she had seen in an animal shelter in Nanaimo. (Our last cat, Dusty had died at age fifteen in 1983).

Laying all aside, we drove to have a look. She was right. This was a full-size tabby, perhaps fourteen months old. Her face was strikingly beautiful, with dark stripes radiated outward from bright yellow-green eyes. Adopting the cat took no convincing. We brought her home, where she quickly devoted herself to both of us.

After considering various names, we settled on Kitty.

Kitty became my close associate in the daily design process. I'd sometimes be faced with a difficult decision or lost in a mathematical maze and turn and ask her what she thought. Her eyes would meet mine. Wisely, she was never quick to answer.

Working with numbers is like taking a continual exam. I'd go upstairs and play around on Rachel's piano for mental relief.

Piano, in *my* case, meant simply playing tunes learned in teenage years from classmates in high-school days, or things picked out by ear. One might think that my being able to play more than one brass instrument, or singing in the choir, or learning music theory in college, and coming from a musical family would have helped. It probably did.

Piano was easy for Rachel. She had taken lessons starting from early childhood. She could look at notes on a page, and they'd come out her fingers. With me, then age fifty-four, except for knowing where middle C was, nothing on a score related to the other eighty-seven keys on a piano.

This was perhaps the busiest time in my life, yet for some reason, it seemed the best time to learn piano. I borrowed a copy of *Thompson Piano Book One* from Petunia and started on page one. Talk about humbling; there's no faking. Practice sounded like a child. Knowing my practicing would drive Rachel to frustration, I bought an electronic piano and earphones, so only I could hear.

Our granddaughter, Juliana, who was about three at the time, was with us for a weekend. We often drew pictures together. At some point during one of those days, I sat on the piano bench, put the earphones on, and began my daily practice. She watched my fingers on the keys for a long time and continued to study what I was doing. Then she said something. I stopped and removed the earphones and bent down to hear her. He face appeared uncomfortably awkward—almost ashamed about something. I asked her to tell me again what she had said.

She looked down at her feet and said, "It's not working, Grandpa."

MY DESIGN WORK was completed in 1994. Vancouver naval architect Robert Harris checked and verified things and assisted with weight studies. To be doubly sure all was correct, numbers were fed into a computer.

Computer modeling was both extensive and expensive. All I needed was to confirm that my calculations were correct, in terms of center of gravity, center of buoyancy, and stability. The resulting summary included all of that and more.

I brought the summary publication to a gathering of the Coastal Missions Society directors and showed it to Roger Parrish, a master mariner. I was sure he would find it interesting.

Roger thumbed through the pages with a puzzled look and muttered something like, "I guess I'm supposed to know about this stuff." Then he asked, "Do you understand it?"

"Well, I understand what I *need* to know, but the rest is over my head."

Roger, knowing it was a pricey packet, asked, "What are you going to say in the meeting?"

I shook my head. "I don't know."

When it came to that part in the meeting, I held the study in my hand and said, "I'll pass this around." And then added, "It speaks for itself."

The aluminum pilothouse was fabricated at Joshua Enterprises in Calgary, Alberta, completed in the Coastal Missions Society's shop, and transported to Victoria, where it was joined to the hull.

Even after initial fabrications began, I continued on the drafting table with cabinetry and lesser details. I also put on coveralls from time to time to lend a hand or give direction.

Volunteers Drew and Margaret Gillespie began constructing air vents to be fitted on top of the pilothouse. Drew, although skilled with wood and cabinetry, had never done anything for a marine application.

All things were precisely detailed on drawings. When completed, those forward-facing vents, port and starboard, would be as tall as a man's shoulder. They were to have a curved back and an angled base to match the camber of the pilothouse.

It all looked cockeyed to Drew. To him, it seemed absurd not to use a square or level. When finished, however, he was thrilled with his accomplishment and was eager to move on to the next challenge.

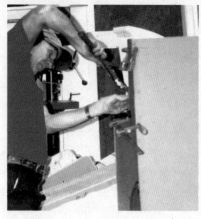

One day while at the drafting table, a phone call came from Jim Fullerton. I had met the man, a composed elderly fellow. He explained that he was a retired pattern maker and wanted to make the new ship's (steering) wheel.

Of all things made of wood, I thought to myself, *it would take the expertise of a pattern maker to do the job.*

"Sure, Jim," I said. "I'll get a drawing to you."

Our conversation continued. Jim spoke of his advanced age and failing health, which was his way of saying, "Please hurry." He went on to explain that he had a special chunk of oak saved for the job, and that he'd *always* wanted to make a ship's wheel.

I laid everything aside and immediately began designing it—no easy task. A ship's wheel is much more than an ornament. It is part of the steering system—hydraulic in this case. It has to be enormously strong; two or three persons might simultaneously grab it, in the case of an excessive roll of the ship in a seaway.

The good news was that the ship's wheel was flawlessly put together. The bad news—if one thinks of going to heaven as bad news—is that Jim died before *Coastal Messenger* ever touched the water. The wheel was displayed beside his casket at his service.

Of the many drawings carefully prepared to build the ship, one was called *The Tabasco Rack.* It was to go on the galley table to hold salt, pepper, jam, sugar cubes, etc., as well as a bottle of Tabasco. A Tabasco bottle was carefully measured to get the drawing exactly right. I had intended to give the job of making it to Jim after he finished the wheel, but at the last, he was so spent that I didn't. Maybe I should have. To this day, that little rack has *never* happened.

Coastal Missions' people continued work on constructions. Brian Burkholder and Tom Maxie were involved daily at the Jenkins worksite. The company that had welded up the aluminum pilothouse gave Coastal Missions a pickup truck to aid their commute. Much went on behind the scenes: Petunia did a lot of the errands and other running around, and headed most business transactions; Anne Burkholder was on bookkeeping; and Gloria Troll made sure there were plenty of cookies and other goodies to keep the Jenkins guys sugared up for best efficiencies.

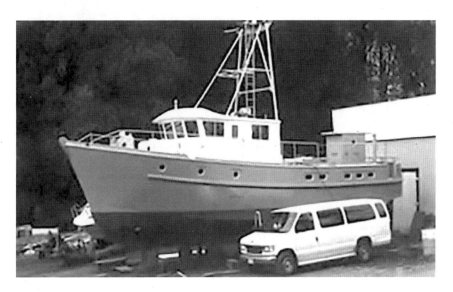

It was while the new *Coastal Messenger* was being built that Rachel retired after twenty-five years at Malaspina College. She was suddenly thrust into office work at the Coastal Missions Society, which was not a retirement job where she could sit back and relax.

Of the Jenkins workforce, steel work was done by Tim Depue and assisted by Johnny West. Dave Critchley, highly qualified marine electrician, did the wiring. Brian Kelly kept track of the Jenkins end of business, and in the long of things, Coastal Missions Society became forever friends with the Jenkins people, especially owners John and Estelle Jenkins.

While all this was happening, Coastal Missions hired somewhat of a genius named John Daly, a man who well understood hydraulics and endless other things. In one case, he converted a wood splitter, by adding pistons and some other appendages into a tool for bending steel into the most useful stairs ever seen in any vessel. The log splitter was then modified a second time to shape stainless steel handrails around the deck.

John Daly

Another friend of the Coastal Missions Society was Ron Pollock. He had a home but often wandered the streets of Victoria. He said that his hobby was people, and that was true, but he also had a hobby of collecting stuff. It was amazing the things that people gave him, and much of what he collected he brought to Coastal Missions. If it was pieces of steel, I told him, "Just throw it on the bank beside the welding shop." Something thrown there was used almost every day.

One day, he arrived with a pickup load of white oak, explaining that some guys were remodeling a McDonald's restaurant and were "just throwing it out." When he asked them about the oak, they said, "It's yours, if you take it away."

His several loads of oak were piled in a dry place, out of the way. Ron McKee went through the pile and methodically removed staples. The shop's planer was used to shave off the old varnish, making the wood like new.

The finished interior of the ship was to be plain and bright, so surfaces were spray painted with coats of melamine white. The final interior was open and tastefully trimmed with (you guessed it) McDonald's oak.

Noise control is part and parcel of boat building. In this case, the vessel's engine would be below the pilothouse. Standard practice for controlling noise was to make a sandwiched pilothouse floor, using three-quarter-inch plywood covered with felt, then a layer of sheet lead, then another layer of felt, and finally a top layer of three-quarter-inch plywood.

When I went to a fabric store and told the lady what I was doing, she began rolling out the specified amount of white felt, which was what she had the most of—colour didn't matter.

A lady customer, with an "I have the right to know" expression on her face, emerged from the great maze of fabric bolts and stood watching the sales clerk measuring out the great amount of felt. When she realized I was the customer, she looked accusingly at me and demanded, "What are you doing with all that felt?"

I said, "I'm making a big white bunny."

Trek to the Sea

THE ALMOST COMPLETE *Coastal Messenger* was standing proudly on blocks at the Jenkins yard near the Victoria General Hospital when Susan Down, from Victoria's *Times Colonist*, arrived with photographer Ray Smith. Her article with Ray's photo appeared in the *Colonist* a few days later. It was a concise article about Coastal Missions, and also announced the imminent launch of the ship.

Sometime between Susan's visit and the day the article was published on September 8, 1998, Brian started the engine and activated the hydraulic system. I stood on the foredeck and began spooling in the anchor rode, which was piled in the bed of a pickup truck—three hundred feet of Samson braid, one hundred fifty feet of half-inch chain, with a one hundred fifty-pound Forfjord anchor at the end.

Remember, the vessel was three or four miles from the sea.

I had never operated that winch except when testing it on the shop floor in Chemainus, yet for some reason, the operation seemed most normal. Spooling was stopped when the drum was nearly full. I walked to the peak and looked down into the bed of the truck, and seeing only a few feet of chain and the anchor remaining, I returned to the controls and brought the anchor up until it nested on its roller, as if it had *always* lived there.

The day came when the ship was to be transferred from its blocking to the beams of a very stout boat-moving trailer. It was an all-day process. A special license was granted to move *Coastal Messenger* on public roads, which had to be done in the wee hours.

Trailer wheels began to move at 2:00 a.m., September 10, 1998. *Coastal Messenger's* four-legged mast would be transported separately.

It was all quite the spectacle in the night: the vessel standing high on its trailer with generator running and portable lights blazing to make everything highly visible. A vehicle with flashing lights led the parade, and a loaded gravel truck was cabled some distance behind, to be sure the loaded trailer could not overpower the towing vehicle on the slant of road leading downward from the Jenkins hill. A "Wide Load" vehicle with bright strobes brought up the rear.

Every part of moving the ninety-something-thousand pounds of steel *Coastal Messenger* in the dark was done in slowest motion.

The procession followed local roads to the main thoroughfare. All had been calculated, measured, and recalculated, but there remained a question of whether *Coastal Messenger* could actually pass under the large steel girders where two lanes of highway crossed. The trailer was guided to the far left, the place of maximum clearance. Everything was then brought to a stop and measurements were taken again. Yes, it *should* pass under, but even so, there remained a question. The procession inched forward, and with less than a handbreadth to spare, the pilothouse brow passed under the first, second, then third, and finally the fourth girder.

A police car with an array of flashing lights was positioned across the highway near the doughnut shop just beyond the Six Mile Pub. The pub had closed, but the doughnut place was alive with customers. Alerted by the commotion, patrons streamed out to watch the unlikely sight of a big boat going down the street. One might have asked what was in that last drink.

All wheels came to a stop at the Department of Defense launching ramp at Esquimalt. The actual launching was put on hold until high tide the next afternoon.

Air was filled with happy anticipation as people gathered for the occasion. People from the Jenkins Yard were excused from work to see the launching. Many brought spouses. Coastal Missions' women had provided a generous picnic.

News cameras arrived and were soon focused on John Jenkins and me, as we were positioned to cut into the special celebration cake.

John asked quietly, "What are we supposed to be doing?"

"Nothing," I prompted. "Just look charming for the pictures." Then I explained, "Today is just the picnic and the launching. A full commissioning will happen in April."

The tide was almost in. It was time to launch. Brian and a small contingent climbed to the deck of *Coastal Messenger* as the towing vehicle maneuvered the trailer to the top of the ramp. After a length of cable was attached to the loaded gravel truck, the towing vehicle backed the trailer to the ramp's incline. When the cable to the gravel truck came up tight—now taking the full weight—the towing vehicle disconnected and moved out of the way.

Next, only by the cable, the gravel truck carefully allowed the trailer, with its great weight, to slowly ease down the incline.

Everyone was standing off to the side, silently watching, and this included the military person Petunia had dealt with when making arrangements for use of the launching ramp. His son Christopher, who was maybe four years old, stood between his father's knees.

A small tug was standing by to assist when the vessel floated free.

Except for the low idling tug's engine and the groans from the heavy gravel truck's brakes, there were no sounds. Tiny wavelets began lapping under the stern of *Coastal Messenger,* and moments later, it floated free.

Everyone continued to stand in silence. Then little Christopher's piercing voice suddenly announced, "IT'S A BOAT!"

Everyone suddenly began laughing, shouting, and clapping.

Brian started the engine, backed the vessel out into the deep, and motored across to the assigned float. Over the next days, the four-legged mast was brought and put in place.

It was during those days that the Coastal Missions Society had two different visitors from Japan just days apart. The first, Fumiko (pronounced Humiko), enjoyed time with Coastal Missions' people at the mission base, and I also took her to Esquimalt to see the new mission vessel.

Certain security measures existed to get into the dockyard. Hard hats were required, and I had a white one for Fumiko. Coastal Missions' white van was a "regular" at the gate, and the security person readily waved us through. We parked close to *Coastal Messenger.*

It was a nice day. Fumiko followed as I stepped on board.

Electrician Dave Critchley was working on wiring that related to mast things. I introduced Fumiko. He graciously acknowledged her.

Yoshiko, the other Japanese friend, arrived to visit Coastal Missions some days later, and like a repeat, I took her to the dockyard, and when nearing security, she put the white hard hat on and we were waved through the gate. Dave was still on mast wiring when I introduced Yoshiko.

"Yes," he said, "I met her a few days ago."

The new *Coastal Messenger* left Esquimalt and came home to its berth at nearby Crofton Harbour near the end of September. After some last details, final adjustments, and rigorous trials, the vessel was ready to start life.

Daughter of the City

COASTAL MESSENGER LEFT Crofton on January 13, 1999, for places south to Olympia, Washington. This was the beginning of its first year as a mission vessel on the coast. It proved to be a harsh winter and a test for the new vessel.

At one point, we came out of Deception Pass with strong current on the stern. There was no turning back. Courses were set for Thatcher Pass. The wind was full-gale southeast and extremely rough in Rosario Strait. *Coastal Messenger* continued with reduced throttle as massive waves swept continually past the ship.

Apart from the alarming *appearance* of conditions through the pilothouse windows, the vessel was riding fine. Eventually out of the extreme conditions in Rosarion Strait, we continued to Friday Harbor and tied inside the big floating breakwater.

The storm raged on. Every now and then, a huge gust would rip through the harbor, sounding like a 747 attempting to abort a landing.

Long swells were walking into Friday Harbour, great enough to cause the huge floating breakwater to roll, which was a sight that, when viewed through galley ports, made me feel sick. I closed the curtains.

Coastal Messenger interior

Coastal Messenger returned home on the twenty-sixth of February, and left again with Brian and crew near the end of March, first to Vancouver then to Victoria in time to prepare for its Commissioning Service on the third of April. Being an officially documented Canadian vessel, and having Victoria as its Port of Registry, it was automatically declared to be "a daughter of the city!"

The city assigned free moorage in front of the Empress Hotel, and free everything for the days before and after the celebration.

Several of us from Coastal Missions had taken navigation courses at Camosun in Victoria. Two of the instructors, Captain Brian Silvester and Captain Richard Turpin, were on hand to assist the occasion.

Recalling the classroom, Brian Silvester was always neat and trim, precise, well dressed, and fastidiously organized. He used a chalkboard with yellow chalk, carefully wiping his fingertips after each illustration.

The other captain, whom all simply called Dick, was a heavy man with long-sleeve shirts always half tucked in—a one-of-the-guys sort of fellow. He used the chalkboard too, but in his case, he ended up with yellow on his hands, in his hair, on his face, on his shirt, and in places on his pants where he wiped his hands from time to time.

You could not help but admire the one and love the other. Both were excellent instructors, and on this occasion, both became happily involved preparing the vessel for its commissioning. Dick, who'd put in his years on navy ships, had said in the classroom (more than once) that he'd *never* shine brass again.

He probably never did, but he was also heard to say that he'd never climb a mast again, yet when readying for the service, someone snapped a picture of him standing proudly on the gantry, high atop the mast, after dressing the ship with flags from stem to stern.

Minno Fast had set up a powerful amplification system with big speakers on the pilothouse. They must have been powerful because some weeks later, a fellow who was boarding the passenger ferry *Coho* at its terminal a distance away, told his girlfriend, "I hear Petunia's voice."

Petunia

He was right. After the rousing hymn, "To God be the Glory" was played by the Salvation Army Band, and after Alan Turnbull played "Amazing Grace" on the pipes, as Brian Burkholder raised the Coastal Missions flag on the port yardarm, Petunia took her place at the podium on the deck of *Coastal Messenger*.

Speaking clearly into the microphone, she began introducing persons who had helped bring *Coastal Messenger* into reality. By her elocution, poise, and attire, she could have passed for the queen.

The icing on the occasion was Sherry Chapin, lovely daughter of John and Margaret Woodford, as she readied to christen the vessel. John had been Chairman of the Vancouver Island branch and had suffered the humiliation of Toronto's rejection along with the rest of us. He continued to promote us as long as he lived.

Sherry took the bottle of Canada Dry in hand. Since the *Coastal Messenger* was floating with its bow a distance from the float, she had been instructed to walk up the deck and break the bottle on the anchor, which projected beyond the bow.

The crowd went silent, as (wearing heels) she carefully made her way forward on the deck. With one hand on the forestay and the other on the neck of the bottle, she hauled back, ready to smash it. A loud volley from a snare drum suddenly broke the silence.

Rather than carry through, she stood and waved sweetly across to her mother on the causeway, and in a clear voice, said, "Hi, Mom!" The crowd broke into laughter. At that moment, she swung back and shattered the bottle. This triggered loud cheering and applause as the band went into a lively melody.

Coastal Messenger continued through the remainder of 1999—two hundred sixty days out and away from home, which was typical for the next many years, as Brian Burkholder and I alternated as skippers.

Many stories could be told.

One was on Thursday, July 13, 2000 when *Coastal Messenger* left the floating logging camp at Grace Harbor on Dall Island. After waving goodbyes to those standing on floats, I sounded a long blast on the whistle, which echoed long through the morning air. We carried on to San Lorenzo Islands and anchored in fifteen fathoms.

San Lorenzo is a few little islands off the west coast of Prince of Wales Island. Nobody lives there, but in the summer, many commercial boats go there. They can conveniently fish by day and anchor by night, or if the Pacific wind is too fierce, they can hole up safely.

Don Ludwigson

The vessel *Jadah* came in. Its first maneuvers suggested it would anchor, but then it proceeded cautiously in our direction. Getting closer, it was possible to see the man at its controls; he had a most curious expression on his face. I hailed him and motioned an invitation for him to tie across the broad stern of *Coastal Messenger*.

Don Ludwigson's grizzled beard merged with the shaggy hair of the dog on his lap. Rachel, seeing opportunity in the moment, grabbed her camera and snapped a picture of Don and Lobo.

The visit made an impression with Don, and that fall, he wrote a letter. Not having an address, he simply penciled words across the envelope: "Coast Missionaries, Vancouver Island, Canada," and the letter arrived. Rachel wrote back and sent the picture. He mailed it to a commercial-fishing magazine and won third prize in its photo contest. It appeared in the next month's issue and went out to seafaring and coastal people far and wide.

When Don went to Fish Expo in Seattle that fall, many people he had never met walked up and addressed him by name and asked about Lobo.

By Mystery of Faith

THE YEAR 2005 was Coastal Missions' twenty-fifth and was celebrated in a variety of ways. The "new" *Coastal Messenger* reenacted the circuit taken by the first *Coastal Messenger* twenty-five years earlier.

At the end of that year's voyaging, in December, a distinct smell of hot metal was noted in the engine room. Brian and I removed one of the oil filters from the engine and took it to the shop. We removed its pleated paper element and squeezed the oil out by placing it between two blocks of plywood in a vice.

Flecks of metal could be seen in the paper when held outside in the sunlight. It was obvious that the grand old Rolls Royce marine diesel engine had reached the end of its working life: twenty-seven years in the wooden vessel and another seven in the new steel one.

It was hard to know what engine could possibly replace that close-to-perfect Rolls Royce marine diesel engine, but after much study, we ordered a new John Deere 6081AFM marine diesel, with a 3.958:1 ZF marine transmission. When an order such as that is placed, one must specify which side the starter is to be on, which side the oil filler and dipstick is to be, and even the colour of the engine—in this case, white.

new engine

While waiting for it to be readied, I worked from the manufacture's blueprints and drew up engine mounts, and Duncan Iron Works fabricated them. Any such installation is a big job; the new engine with its marine transmission was lowered into the ship on February 15, 2006. Everything fit perfectly.

A new console with John Deere gauges was made and wired in, and circuits were activated and tested. Again, all worked perfectly.

When we first announced that the old Rolls Royce had come to its end and the vessel would have to be repowered, one of the directors had questions. He seemed troubled about cost, so I assured him by saying that I would do the engineering and Brian would head installation. The costs would therefore be greatly minimized. Even so, he seemed distressed.

The new engine installation went smoothly, except for struggles with suppliers of some exhaust system parts, but that also came together nicely.

The last completion was to align the engine to the shaft; a laser devise was used to flawlessly do that.

The day came when the starter button was pushed and the engine burst to life. Trial runs were made. All aspects of the installation were rigorously tested, and somehow, by the mystery of faith and the encouraging support of many, combined with the outcomes of God, all costs were met.

Soon after, provisions were placed on board and everything was put away. The ship was spotless, inside and out. The beds were made and spirits were typically high. Tom Maxie, master of marine enamels and excellent in all areas of ship cosmetics, had the vessel looking like new.

All was ready, and Brian was in his place in the pilothouse with engine idling, while I stood with the little crowd on the float to say goodbye. The lines were then cast off, and *Coastal Messenger* maneuvered sweetly away from the float and was off to pick up its place on the circuit calendar.

I turned to leave with the others and noted that there were tears in the eyes of the doubting director. So, I stepped over beside him with a reassuring smile, saying something about the great abilities of the team. He looked down and quietly confessed, "I didn't understand. I just didn't understand."

That was years ago.

I continued as skipper on *Coastal Messenger*, each year covering the great circuit on the British Columbia coast, and south in Washington, and as far north as Sumner Strait, Alaska.

My last run was on October 20, 2017, ending at Campbell River. I was seventy-eight then, and my worn-out back and partially crippled legs were making me less and less safe around the water.

The vessel continued with Brian Burkholder and crew, as scheduled, and ended that year of voyaging on the fourth of December. *Coastal Messenger* continued on a one-skipper schedule into the following years, and is (in fact) out there right now.

As for "new" *Coastal Messenger's* accomplishments to date, it has traveled the equivalent distance of around the globe three times— once with the old Rolls Royce, and just short of twice with the John Deere.

As for me, I continued as president and superintendent of the work until Chet McArthur took over in April 2018—a good move, since you may remember that I allowed my name to stand *only temporarily* ... to get things rolling back in 1980.

Memories and Happenings

THIS BRINGS US to the last chapter, and somewhat of a replay of events. Meaningful life started when I stepped out of the pages of Oregon and onto the deck of *Gleaner*, headed for Alaska in 1949. The next twenty-three years of my life were packed with a huge array of experiences and memory makers: *Gleaner* life, fish traps and pirates, Ketchikan newspapers, Victor the seal, village life, junior-high awkwardness, and later, high school, college, army, married and young family life, boat shop, Boeing aircraft, more boat shop, Alaska tidal wave, tugs, and more tugs, Cook Inlet, family cruising, and Nanaimo. Vancouver Island finally felt like home.

Those seven years with the Vancouver Island branch of the Shanymen in the 1970s was a preparation. Feeling the need for a proper vessel and a team of workers were part of it. When at its highest point of happenings, I asked Petunia what she saw to be the long-term future of Pachena. She thought about my question for a long time, and then said, "I see Pachena as a very small dot on a very large map."

No one at the time could have predicted that someone would come from Toronto and bring Pachena to a stop. But the call of the coast and conscience of the team was great—great enough to rally with even greater force, and has continued these past forty years, while Pachena has indeed become a very small dot on a very large map.

For the record, and going back to my memory of the pier at Muchalat Inlet in 1972, and seeing the need for a proper mission vessel and longing for a solid team, Coastal Missions started with eight fully involved workers: George Loewen, Brian Burkholder, Ron and Joan McKee, Anne Spencer, Debbie Forney, Gloria Troll, and me.

Tom Maxie, who had been earlier involved at Pachena, returned to full-time participation 1981, and Chet and Teresa McArthur, who both trained at Pachena, returned to full involvement after raising a family. Rachel was always a part of it too, and able to join in fully after retiring from teaching in 1997.

All of those listed above who are still alive remain in the work as I type this, forty years later: Chet and Teresa McArthur, Brian and Anne Burkholder, Petunia (widowed in 2001 and now married to my also widowed brother Frank), Tom and Debbie Maxie, and Rachel and me.

Yes, there is some truth in saying one whiff of ocean air mixed with the smell of diesel smoke set the course for the rest of my life on God's big coast.

GOD'S BIG COAST
ROY GETMAN

Learned and Gained

WRITING THIS BOOK has been quite an exercise. Being a life-long forward-facing fellow, recalling the past was a challenge. Memory went back briefly to a time when I was about four and to a little creek that filled a shallow pond behind the shed near our Dixie Mountain home. It was a good place to float twigs and leaves, and the dirt beside it was soft, and I could make little roads—the extent of my small world.

I was the youngest, and at that time in history—what with the war going on—everyone was much too busy to be fussing over a little boy. Our closest neighbors were miles away. I was scarcely aware that we had any. What a contrast—my circle likely comprises a few thousand people today.

Now in octogenarian years, I better see how many of my most significant gains were born out of hurts, disappointments, bad happenings, and hardships.

My most practical and useful advice came from the Book of Proverbs: "Trust in the Lord with all your heart and lean not on your own understanding; in all your ways acknowledge Him and He will direct your paths." Looking back, I see that, in spite of whimsical me, those words are my story, and the yield of that leading has brought meaning to me and to the lives of many.

The Book Project

MOST PEOPLE KNOW that committing oneself to writing a book is a big project. But then what? I contacted FriesenPress through their website. A short time later, my phone rang, and it was a real person to give realistic and encouraging direction—a first taste of the support that was there through the publishing process.

One can never know how fulfilling writing is until actually carrying through.

Printed in Canada